12/11/04

SLEEPING ON POTATOES

For our wonderful
Neighbors, Carol & David
with my Compliments

Carl Nomura

KCN@Cablespeed.com

SLEEPING ON
POTATOES

*A LUMPY ADVENTURE
FROM MANZANAR TO THE
CORPORATE TOWER*

Carl Nomura

Erasmus Books

Bellingham, Washington

Library of Congress Card Number: 2003108043

Nomura, Carl
Sleeping on Potatoes: A Lumpy Adventure from
Manzanar to the Corporate Tower / by Carl Nomura

ISBN 0-970-1947-3-0 (paperback acid-free paper)

Cover: Carl Nomura as a boy. Book designed by Katherine Yurica.

To Robert Frost for his poem, *The Road Less Traveled* and to Abraham Maslow for his studies on *Self-Actualized* people. Though their ideas caused me to do many things the "hard way," they showed me how to have a more fulfilling and adventurous life.

And to my mother, Mizuko who advised, "If you have a good idea, use it, sell it, give it away or throw it away, but never keep it and do nothing with it. If you did nothing, you'd keep thinking about that one idea and never get a new one."

CONTENTS

CONTENTS

CONTENTS

CONTENTS

PREFACE

As I wandered through life, sometimes with a purpose and sometimes without, I encountered many situations that I thought were important enough to share with others. These experiences with family, friends, colleagues, and animals stuck in my memory. I wanted to write about them.

Writing has always been important in my work. I wrote scientific articles when I was a scientist, and white papers and memos when I was in management. When I retired making the transition from the cold and inert world of science and business to the warm and pleasant ambiance of an artists' community, I figured the time had come to write about my experiences.

I began writing these stories about twelve years ago, attempting from the outset to write in simple language. My computer says I made it: the book has a low fog factor, which means that only an elementary grade level of education is required to understand it.

My original idea was to write a series of short stories. Only recently did I realize that I had the makings of an autobiography. I have tried, to the best of my ability, to tell it like it was but I admit that, when the outcome was boring, I lied. And you'll never find out where. I also changed the names of several people to protect their privacy.

The name of the book, *Sleeping on Potatoes*, is the title of one of my stories. It is also a metaphor for the bumpy and lumpy ride I had in my formative years. Surprisingly, I still love potatoes even though I ate little else for many months. Thus the potatoes become a private metaphor of how delicious life has been for me. The book celebrates the good things and events that have filled my life, with some tough years sandwiched in between. Though I didn't succeed all the time, I tried to be modest. So I am not the hero of this tale.

I didn't realize I had reached the end of the book until I ran out of ideas. I thought, "I need more adventures to continue writing. I've exhausted everything that I can remember." Then, for a few years, I was in the "creeping elegance" stage where I wrote little and spent most of my time editing the text. Finally I stopped fiddling with it and declared the book finished.

And here it is, warts and all. I hope you like it.

ACKNOWLEDGMENTS

I began the craft of writing by taking a creative writing course from Phyllis Miletich who encouraged me with the words, "Tell me. Truly. Do you really enjoy writing all this stuff? It's dull as dirty dish water."

I shaped up and began writing stuff that met her approval. Subsequently, through her coaching, many of my friends began to encourage me to publish my stories.

I belonged to several writing groups, but the one that was longest lasting and most effective met every week for about three hours. We read our compositions out loud and received and gave suggestions. The other members of the group: Audrey McConachie, Patricia Perreault, Les Smith and Kathleen Beck are published and expert writers. They all became my mentors and friends.

Another mentor is Patricia Wight who read and critiqued every story, then suggested that I might group them into themes.

Poetry has always mystified me. I just didn't understand it. Carol Light taught me to understand the essence of poetry. I had been missing many allusions and metaphors because I was not sufficiently schooled in the classics such as Shakespeare, the Bible and myths. I had too many differential equations in my head. But I learned to appreciate masterpieces such as how smoothly the Queen of the fairies in *A Midsummer Night's Dream* orated in perfect iambic pentameter.

My daughter, Teri Nomura, read and commented on several versions of the manuscript. She paid particular attention to the accuracy of the stories about family members.

Gwen Moore persuaded me to publish the book and then volunteered to organize the book. She furthermore suggested that it be written as a memoir. She wanted me to write the connecting stories such as the war years, the family, the Army and my work so that readers would know who is who and that the book as a whole would make sense. Her suggestions were monumental.

I thank Katherine Yurica, publisher of Erasmus Books, who

ACKNOWLEDGMENTS

was the first to urge me to continue writing my stories more than ten years ago. She visualized me as a little boy experiencing the wonders of the world and then growing up. Not only was she first to influence me but she is also the last since she published the book.

Finally, I thank all my teachers, friends, children, neighbors, dogs and cats for helping me put this book together.

SLEEPING ON POTATOES

CHAPTER I

Family

THE ROLL OF A BOTTLE

Deer Lodge, Montana

In 1927, at dinner with his family, my father, Kazuichi Nomura, was stunned to see a bottle rolling across the table toward him. According to an old Japanese superstition, this was a sign that he was going to die three years hence. My father was fifty-one years old and in good health, but from that moment on he was preparing for his own death. As part of this, he decided that he must have his entire family around him when he died. It was this self-interest that prompted him to order my older brothers and sister home from Japan.

Then, when he had everyone together, he began to agonize over the future. He told his wife, "My children have no one to marry. We must go where there are many Japanese people. We will move to California."

My father was a stern, uncompromising man, with a ferocious temper and a childish temperament. My mother, Mizuko

Takahashi Nomura, long-since resigned to his tyrannical ways, said nothing, but began to plan the move.

MY MOTHER MIZUKO'S STORY

Hiroshima, Japan

In 1601, the Takahashi family moved from Kyoto to Hiroshima. We know this because the Takahashis played an important role in Hiroshima history, and their family history, going back for thirty-two generations, has been kept on scrolls stored at a temple.

Once in Hiroshima, they built a home by the ocean. And then began the massive, generations-long task of filling the ocean shore with rocks and dirt from the mountain. As soon as a new area became viable, it was turned into farmland. After 300 years of toil, the Takahashi family had a vast estate with acreage stretching into the man-made seacoast.

It was the custom in Japan that, in each generation, the oldest son inherited everything. In the generation before my mother's, there were three sons. My mother's father, Kichinosuke, was the third, and therefore a very unlikely heir. This meant he would never be wealthy, but that did not concern him. This circumstance gave him the freedom he felt wealth would deny him.

Kichinosuke was a widower, having lost his first wife only a year after their marriage. Now he married the beautiful daughter of a well-to-do family that owned a coal mine. The family made only one demand of him: that he agree to sign a pledge stating that, if their mining business ran into financial difficulties, he would be responsible for their debts.

Kichinosuke was a man who believed in himself and his own resources. He signed the pledge without giving it a second thought.

As a third son, he could not imagine that this decision would cause him grief.

Then, quite unexpectedly, his oldest brother died. The death of this wonderful young man was a great sorrow to the family. Then they realized that the estate would now pass to the second son. But this son was a scholar who, when informed of his inheritance, refused it. He passed his newly acquired wealth to Kichinosuke and went to Tokyo to pursue his dream of becoming a philosopher and teacher. (In Hiroshima, there is today a twice life-sized statue of this man, my granduncle.)

So it was that the estate fell to Kichinosuke. He was now the wealthiest man in town with servants, field hands, overseers, cooks, and even amahs for the children. Since he was a rare college graduate, he was chosen to be principal of the school and, later, the mayor of the town. People paid much respect to him as well as to all members of his family, and his family prospered. Indeed, in 1936, the Emperor of Japan awarded him the Order of the Chrysanthemum for fifty years of public service. My mother Mizuko, third of four children, was born in 1895. In later years, she recalled being embarrassed by the townspeople bowing when greeting her and calling her *ojoosan* (meaning honorable young lady).

Mizuko lived her early years in the lap of luxury. But when she was seven, disaster struck the family: the mine owned by her mother's family went bankrupt. This was the coal mine for which Kichinosuke had pledged his financial support.

My grandfather soon realized that not only had the mine failed, but that, in the process, it had also generated an enormous debt. He promised to assume the burden of that debt, and he was determined to honor that promise. First he sold his properties. The most valuable asset was the land that went far out into the sea. But still that wasn't enough. Finally he was forced to sell the two-hundred-year-old family mansion. The structure was made with wooden pegs instead of nails. Thus it was possible to dismantle it, move the pieces away, and reassemble it somewhere else. The grief of the Takahashi family on seeing their home being dismantled can only be imagined.

Meanwhile, they moved into the tiny guesthouse, which was meant to house only a small number of infrequent visitors. They were poor, but the family still retained their high status in the community.

There was yet another blow to the family when Mizuko's mother, overwhelmed by events, died of grief. Mizuko turned to her loving grandmother, Takahashi, for comfort. This kind woman pampered the young girl and allowed her to be spoiled, a luxury she would never enjoy again. The grandmother would hide candy in her sleeve and tease Mizuko to find the prize.

But, when Mizuko was twelve, tragedy struck again. Her grandmother died, leaving Mizuko with no protector.

Her father cared about her, but his first thought now was to find himself a new wife. He had outlived two wives already, and, with his current financial woes, he couldn't afford to be too picky.

The third wife became Mizuko's undoing, for this woman was abrasive, critical and jealous of Mizuko's close relationship with her father. In a small house, it was almost impossible for her to avoid this difficult woman.

When Mizuko turned fifteen, her stepmother decided that the easiest way to get the young woman out of the house was to arrange a marriage for her. But this proved to be no easy matter for Mizuko had grown very tall and was now five feet six. That made her a full head taller than most of the undernourished Japanese men at the turn of the century.

Mizuko was a very good student, and her father wanted her to go to medical school. But she cast aside such ideas because she was overcome with the desire to get away from her stepmother and the tiny people of Japan.

She heard that in America everyone was tall. Armed with that information, she decided she must marry someone who was going to America.

MY FATHER KAZUICHI'S STORY

Seattle, Washington

As luck would have it, Kazuichi Nomura, a widower with two children, just arrived in Hiroshima. He made the journey to Japan from the United States in search of a Japanese wife.

Kazuichi Nomura, the first son in his family, was born on New Year's Day, 1876, in Hiroshima, Japan. His parents named him Kazuichi, written in Chinese characters with two horizontal lines ("one one") and meaning "number one." From the beginning, he was loaded down with high expectations.

Kazuichi, like Mizuko, came from a family of teachers. But he did not follow in their footsteps. Perhaps the loss of his mother, who died when he was two years old, caused others in the family to over-indulge him. In any case, he became a spoiled brat and dropped out of school.

This pampered child grew up to be a playboy with skills in dancing, singing, gambling and drinking. He developed none of the qualities needed to become a good husband or parent. He remained a child into adulthood with a great distaste for work.

Kazuichi's family had moved to Washington where they settled near Seattle. Eventually he leased a farm, married, and became the father of two young daughters. It was the death of his first wife that prompted him to return to Hiroshima in 1910.

When he arrived, he immediately hired a marriage broker and laid out his requirements for a new wife. The broker introduced him to the Takahashi family with the proposal that Mizuko become his wife. She had become so distressed with her situation that she agreed to marry Kazuichi even though she had only caught a fleeting glance of him.

After their arrival in Seattle, Mizuko learned that Kazuichi left his two daughters, Chioko who was four, and the infant Shigeko in Japan with his deceased wife's sister. He promised this poor woman he would send support money, but he never did, leaving the girls to fend for themselves as unwanted children.

Another shock awaited Mizuko. She soon discovered that Kazuichi had not brought her to his vegetable farm to be his beloved wife, but rather to be his workhorse. There was a clear division of labor: she was to work the farm, and he would sell the produce. In other words, he wanted nothing to do with the farm work, and Mizuko was left to fend for herself.

My father spent most of his days drinking and gambling in town. Once in a while he worked on a business deal. He would, for example, contract to buy a field of corn that was almost ripe. Then he would arrange to have it harvested and sell the corn. Though he was a third-grade dropout, he knew his math well. He could estimate the value of the corn by counting rows, the number of plants per row, and the average number of ears per stalk. He made the calculations in his head and then made the offer.

Kazuichi was very successful in his ventures, so much so that he could afford to take eight lavish vacations to Japan. He always traveled alone, leaving Mizuko and the children behind.

MIZUKO'S NEW LIFE

Meanwhile, Mizuko was forced to make the difficult transition from nursemaid and schoolgirl to country farm laborer. She worked hard and was soon adept at farm work. But it was difficult for a proud girl to accept her change of status.

She became a pioneer woman, felling trees, pulling out the stumps to make farmland, doing all of the farm work. (As a teenager, I recall being impressed with her skill at harnessing and working with horses. She knew how to plow a straight line with a team of horses.)

When Kazuichi came home from the market with his wagon, he expected Mizuko to run immediately to the gate to open it. If she failed, he crashed through the gate, leaving her to fix it. As soon as he got into the house, he expected the food to be hot and either on the table or in transit. If it wasn't, he overturned the table and demanded instantaneous recovery.

Mizuko was left to do everything on her own: the farm chores, the housecleaning, shopping, and cooking. Kazuichi even went so far as to refuse to arrange for a doctor or midwife to be with her when it was time to deliver her first child. She hadn't menstruated until she was eighteen, and so didn't become pregnant until the third year of her marriage.

Mizuko had never seen animals giving birth, and certainly no one had ever explained the process to her. At eighteen, she was ignorant of her own anatomy and the birthing process frightened her out of her wits.

But somehow she managed to deliver her first son all by herself. Years later, she told us, "When I started pulling out the placenta, I wondered if it was attached to me inside."

She named the baby *Takuma*, for he had been born in Tacoma, but as with most of us, he later adopted an English name. I knew him as Henry.

My mother went about her farm chores with Henry strapped to her back. She used to tell us about the time when Kazuichi entrusted her with a twenty dollar gold piece. He asked her to keep it safe for him and she put it carefully in the pocket of her dress. But when she returned to the house after working all day in the field, she realized it was missing. It must have fallen out of her pocket while she was working.

Mizuko was frantic. With Henry strapped to her back, she examined every head of cabbage, working late into the night by the light of a lantern. Her greatest fear was facing her husband's wrath, a confrontation that would inevitably end in a beating. She never forgot the joy she felt when she found that gold piece.

Henry was followed three years later by the birth of another boy, *Jiro*, who was to be known as Sam. Again, she delivered her baby all by herself, a performance she would repeat for all but her sixth child.

Mizuko believed having his own sons would soften Kazuichi's heart. She couldn't have been farther from the truth. Kazuichi didn't want his sons around. Children were demanding. They cramped his style. And he knew how to get rid of them.

He waited until 1920, when Sam was four and Henry seven, to act. He wrote to my mother's younger sister and asked her to take the boys. The sister replied that she couldn't handle more children, that she was already overwhelmed. She was only twenty-two, with a newborn of her own and a stepson to look after. But my canny father wrote back promising lavish support money. My aunt's husband was a poorly paid schoolteacher, and the money sounded like the answer to her prayers. Sure that they would lead much better lives with an increased income, she readily agreed to take the boys.

My father then planned one of his vacation flings in Japan, and told the boys they were to come with him. He took the boys straight to his sister-in-law's house. She welcomed them into her home, sure that everything would work out for the best.

How little she knew my father: Once he was rid of Henry and Sam, he forgot all about them, neither writing nor sending a penny. For eight years, all the thanks my aunt received were embarrassed letters of apologies from my mother who suffered much anguish, but could do nothing because of her tyrannical husband.

Thus my two older brothers, like their half-sisters, truly were unwanted children. In later years, Henry used to talk about how he had tried to eat as little as possible at meals to minimize his burden on the family. And Sam recalled, "I used to be an honor student with a good memory. I was able to recite verbatim, thirty-minute speeches given by the principal. Then I got sick and ran a high fever for a long time. No one took care of me, and the fever just ran on and on. When I recovered, I couldn't remember anything at all."

After depositing the two boys with Mizuko's sister, Kazuichi decided to visit the two daughters he left behind eight years before. There he encountered a violently angry ex-sister-in-law. She absolutely refused to care for Chioko for one more day. She packed up the thirteen-year-old and told Kazuichi to take her home to America. She did, however, want to keep the younger sister, Shigeko, because she had become a valuable milk delivery girl for the Nomura's dairy.

By the time Kazuichi returned home, there were two daughters in the family. My sister Yoshiko, whom we all call "Yosh," was born just after her brothers were sent into exile.

Chioko sized up her fearsome father and soon decided to become her stepmother's ally. This made life easier for both of them since they were now able to help each other figure out how to deal with him.

Chioko was not five feet tall, fair skinned, with fine features, and she soon blossomed into a beauty. She attracted much attention in this society where the men out-numbered the women by more than twenty to one. Most men were able to acquire wives only by going back to Japan or getting a picture bride. Chioko had many suitors when she was sixteen. From a host of them, she chose Junji Kaneko, a handsome man about fifteen years older than she.

THE RAILROAD YEARS

Deer Lodge, Montana

In 1921, after ten years of farming and with no savings to show for it, my father decided to sell the farm and move on. He heard that good jobs were available working on the railroad. So he moved the family to Deer Lodge, Montana.

My parents were both hired by the railroad. My father, like the other laborers, laid railroad tracks from the west to connect with those being laid from the east.

My family, like everyone else working on the tracks, lived in boxcars fashioned into a warren of bunks. As the tracks were laid, the boxcar homes were rolled forward. This continued until winter came. Then the cars were pulled back to Deer Lodge and into the roundhouse.

I was born in one of those boxcars in April of 1922, somewhere between Deer Lodge and Three Forks. My mother gave me the name Saburo, meaning third son. I might have been called "Sab" for short in later years. But instead, when I was six-months

old, Chioko suggested that my name be changed to Kaworu meaning "fragrance" —not a perfume smell—but rather a masculine
scent to fit my gentle temperament. (I've always hated this name.
My mother assured me it was a good masculine name, but she did
not convince me.) Unable to find work in this male-dominated
environment, my mother cut off her hair, donned a pair of cover-
alls, and landed herself a job as a laborer in the roundhouse. The
railroad engineers got better traction when climbing steep grades
if they sprinkled sand on the tracks. But the sand had to be dry.
Mizuko's responsibility was to shovel sand into the furnace for this
drying process.

It was hard work, and, after I was born, she found it especially
difficult. She was breast-feeding me and lived in fear of being discovered. Then one day the foreman caught her. He was enraged
that a woman had tricked him and fired her on the spot.

The family remained in Deer Lodge for several years, and my
sister Ayako was born in 1926. Meanwhile, Henry and Sam had
been living in an incredibly hostile environment for eight years,
and Shigeko, in her unwelcoming home, for thirteen years.

And then, suddenly, my father decided to bring his family
together. The bottle rolled across a table toward him, and he was
sure he was going to die in three years. He would send for his three
exiled children.

I was five and had never met these siblings, and it was a wonderful surprise to suddenly have two older brothers and another
sister.

But the reunion wasn't so happy for everyone. The other children did not know their father, and he could be incredibly cruel.
Kazuichi always looked angry and he beat members of his family
with or without obvious reasons. Henry became the most frequent
target because, of all things, objects with wheels on them fasci-

nated him. He brought home wheels that he found in trash cans and would spend the day constructing carts from odd pieces of wood. When my father came home, he would fly into a rage, smashing the carts to bits and beating Henry. Kazuichi thought making carts was childish behavior for a fourteen-year-old kid, and he wouldn't stand for it.

Undaunted, Henry continued to make carts, only to have them smashed. Finally he hit on the idea of making a really sturdy cart using a single bed frame. This one was so solid that, when my father jumped on it, he just bounced off with no harm done to the cart.

In frustration, Kazuichi started hitting Henry. But to his great surprise, the kid began to fight back. Silently, we all cheered Henry on, and finally Henry began to win. My father stopped and stared at him. Clearly he had a newfound respect for his son, and he never touched him again.

Henry's fascination with carts was not pointless, for later in life he developed his own successful trucking business.

But Kazuichi neither knew nor cared about his children's dreams for the future. He cared only about his own place in the family history. That was the reason for his autocratic decision to move his family to California. The children must be among Japanese people, they must marry and perpetuate the family history.

CHAPTER II

Growing Up

THE CANNERY

Long Beach, California

So it was that the family moved to Long Beach, California, leaving Chioko and her husband, Junji, in Montana. My parents and the oldest children—Shigeko, Henry, and Sam—found jobs at the local cannery. They spent their days lopping the heads off fish and gutting them. The jobs depended on the catch, so there were days when they had no work at all. Other times they worked day and night for three or four days in a row.

When they were at work, the rest of us had to fend for ourselves. Yosh, who was eight, became our little mother. She washed our clothes, cleaned the house, supervised us, and cooked. On payday, she went to the market for some vegetables and the short ribs, which cost eight cents a pound. From this she made the stock for our week long main dish: soup. As the week passed, she added whatever we could find in the kitchen to the pot. Sometimes we might have a fish, but often there was nothing to add except water.

When payday came around again, Yosh would put in more short ribs and vegetables to bring the stock back to full strength. Yosh seldom washed the pot because it remained in active use most of the time.

NOMURA'S CASH AND CARRY

Los Angeles, California

By 1929, our family had saved enough money to buy a lease on a grocery store at 259 East Twenty-third Street in Los Angeles. We put up a sign over the store—"Nomura's Cash and Carry"—and found ourselves in business.

The city astounded me. I remember standing in front of the store and looking straight up Maple Avenue. Twenty-three blocks away, I could see the City Hall Obelisk. For a kid who'd seen so little of city life, this was a wonderful sight.

The store served both as a source of income and a dwelling. We slept upstairs and the kitchen and dining area were downstairs behind the store. So the nine of us were crammed into what amounted to a two-bedroom apartment.

Still, this far surpassed any accommodations we had had in the past. The yard was spacious but without vegetation of any kind. It was all dirt, which from my perspective was wonderful. Dirt was perfect for playing marbles. We knew how to shoot them accurately and to great distances. Unfortunately, that art has disappeared, but we had a wonderful time.

Our new neighborhood was pleasant and friendly. We had a steady clientele, but most of our neighbors were renters, so it was a constantly shifting customer base. My mother gave them identifiers because she still had a limited command of English. (She spoke to us in Japanese and we responded in broken Japanese.) "Cat Woman" had three or four cats. The man with a mud-colored neurotic poodle was the "Dog Man." Then there was the "Chicken Woman," so-called not because she raised chickens, but rather because she looked like one. Her face sagged so that the folds of skin under her chin looked like wattles. And she dressed as if she were trying to imitate a chicken: her small hat could have passed for a comb on a Rhode Island Red.

One woman, not more than four feet eight and round as a ball, might well have been called "Ball Woman," but mother had already dubbed her "Jewish Woman." These nicknames were, of course, spoken only in Japanese. But they enabled my mother to speed up service by saying, for example, "Please get a can of tomato soup for 'Jewish Woman'."

We were extremely careful to avoid offense with our nicknames, but my mother was horrified to discover that she had regularly offended "Jewish Woman" in a completely different way. One day, when she was totaling the purchases, "Jewish Woman" asked, "What is that you are saying? You keep saying 'Jew' over and over again. Are you saying 'nine Jew, ten Jew'?"

My mother tried to explain that the word "ju," means "ten" in Japanese. She was using it often because it occurs in all Japanese numbers from ten to ninety-nine. To count, she would say, "Juichi, niju, sanjusan yonju go," meaning ten, twenty, thirty and so on.

"Jewish Woman" still seemed annoyed. My mother apologized, and ever after she added all numbers silently, but still in Japanese.

RELIGION

In the beginning, there was nothing. I never heard about God, church or religion until I was five when a family friend took me to a church, probably a Presbyterian one. At the back of the pew facing me was a narrow shelf with a hole in it. In the hole was a tiny vial that held no more than a teaspoon of a purple liquid. My hostess said it was the blood of Christ. I was transfixed by the redness of the blood when, as though by a signal, everyone picked up a vial, stood up and drank. I did likewise and thought it tasted just like sweet grape juice. Then, when two hundred people returned the vials into their holes in the shelves, they did it in such precise unison that it sounded like a gunshot and it was just as loud. I was stunned by the incongruity of the noise where hushed silence prevailed only a moment before.

After the move to Los Angeles, I heard nothing about religion until it was time for me to go to school. My mother held the opinion that the Catholics provided the best education, so she enrolled me in Maryknoll School.

I hated that place with uncontrollable passion. When the bus came, I yelled and screamed. The bus driver had to drag me onto the bus while my mother pushed from behind. This scene was repeated every single morning, and my resolve never weakened.

Eventually, my mother gave up and sent me to St. Vincent, a local parochial school. The girls wore blue uniforms with white collars and the boys donned black ties. I didn't like this school much better, but I got used to it after I acquired some playmates.

My special friend was John Green, who came dressed looking like little Lord Fauntleroy. His face and hands were almost colorless except for the blue veins, which showed through. We wrestled a lot and, by the end of the day, he was so disheveled he no longer looked like a sissy. But the next morning, there he'd be again in his perfect, Fauntleroy attire. He was beautiful.

Sister *Perpetual* was the official disciplinarian of the school. Forty years later I learned that we mispronounced her name. It should have been Perpetua. (Perpetual existed in *Lake Woebegon* but we didn't know that.)

Sister Perpetual was short and fat, and it was impossible to detect a trace of joy or love on her face. She came to class everyday to spank the bad kids. We held out our hands as she beat them with force using an eighteen-inch ruler. She beat the girls on the legs—there must have been a reason for the sexual differentiation in the punishment. She would beat harder and harder until we winced and then hit softly afterwards. We soon learned that it didn't pay to be heroic. We cried out after the first whack. As she worked, her face became flushed and she gasped for air from her aerobic exertion. I wondered if she enjoyed her calling and what she did when she wasn't beating us. We thought her named fitted her because she beat us perpetually.

Certain kids were not punished. One was a child star in the "Our Gang" comedies. He was always acting up, but Sister Monica never noticed his misbehavior. Another one was a girl who came to school in a chauffeur-driven limousine. She was the granddaughter of the major benefactor of St. Vincent. John Crow was never beaten because he had steel braces and could barely move. I thought such uneven treatment was hypocritical.

Once we learned to read, we had to go to school at 7:00 A.M. to learn to sing and to recite the mass. The instructor was a serious and humorless man who looked like an unsmiling Harpo Marx. We sang *Tantum Ergo* and chanted the *mea culpas* like pros but we didn't understand one word. Harpo never bothered to explain what we were reciting. Through daily repetition, we learned to recite the entire mass without conscious effort and in record time

because we by-passed the niceties of intonations and meditative
pauses used by the priests.

Following the lesson, we went to mass. This meant that we
were going to church six days a week. After six years of this regi-
men, I claimed that I didn't have to go to church for the next
thirty years since I had gone to church an average of once a week
in advance.

The aspect of the mass that I enjoyed was the pageantry of
High Mass conducted in Latin. Several years later, when I studied
Latin, I had the pleasure of translating what I had committed to
memory. Now that the vernacular replaces Latin, the mass loses its
luster.

'23 CHEVY

Meanwhile, the store was doing well enough that, in 1928,
my father was able to buy a five-year-old car for thirty-five dollars.
It was a 1923 Chevrolet sedan with wooden-spoke wheels, running boards, and canvas snap-on window shields that were useless
because the aging isinglass was nearly opaque.

My father thought he'd cut a wonderful bargain until the first
time he tried to start the car by himself. The seller demonstrated
the procedure but had been careful to keep the car running so that
father could simply drive it home. He parked it in the driveway
and we all admired it tremendously.

I remember the first time father tried to start it on his own.
The whole family gathered around it to watch. Father was in the
driver's seat and Henry had the honor of being the first to crank.
A single turn of that crank should have started the engine, and
away we should have gone. Instead, when Henry cranked, the

Chevy became a violent monster, bucking and shimmying as if trying to throw its rider. My father, true to his nature, started yelling at Henry.

"What's the matter with you? Are you trying to get us all killed? Let me do that."

But when he tried, the Chevy kicked with even more vehemence. Sam was the one who finally figured it out: the trick was to put the fingers and thumb under the crank handle. That way, when the engine backfired, it didn't break off the thumb. But it was a hard-won lesson and they had the black and blue right arms to prove it.

Once we had the Chevy running, it was pure joy. I remember the first time six of us climbed in for a ride. When we reached the fantastic speed of thirty-five miles an hour, we felt as if we were soaring. Then we came to a railroad crossing and braced ourselves, sure that we were about to be jolted to pieces. Instead, we floated over the tracks without a sound at our break-neck speed. This was the most memorable ride of my life.

My father reached a compromise with the car, and managed, with a good deal of cursing, to get it started. But in 1930, the year after my youngest brother Yoshito was born, he decided it was time for a change. He went to the shop and had a starter installed.

I was eight at the time and I remember thinking it was magic! Push the button on the floor and the engine roared. This was so easy that father soon stopped walking anywhere. He even drove to the corner newsstand. He began to drive farther and farther from home, and before long was driving all over Los Angeles without getting lost. And he did this without assistance from street signs or maps, because he had never learned to read English. Instead, he guided himself with landmarks: turn left at the gas station with a red sign or right at the billboard with the Camel ad.

One summer day he drove us all the way to Long Beach, a

good fifty miles from our home. He parked the car on the beach, and we were all so happy to be on a picnic by the ocean that we didn't notice it was low tide.

When we came back to the car, tired and happy and ready to go home, we found water lapping at the back wheels. My father started the car and tried to drive out, but one wheel spun and was soon buried in the sand right up to the axle.

A small man parked nearby was watching us. Finally he opened his trunk and pulled out a two-by-six. He approached my father and said, "Take this. I'm going to lift the car and when I do, shove this board under the wheel."

"What do you mean, you're going to . . ."

But the man wasn't listening. He took off his shoes and crouched down low with his back against the wheel, reached back to grab the spokes of the wheel and began to lift. As he did so, his feet sank a few inches into the wet sand. But he managed to get the car high enough so that father could shove the board under the wheel.

"Now get in and put the car in first gear," the stranger instructed my father. "And the rest of you come and help shove."

With everyone shoving from behind, we moved the car to the safety of high ground. The stranger shrugged off our thanks, but we were all astounded. My five-feet-eight brothers and father towered over his no more than five-feet-two frame, and he couldn't have weighed more than a hundred pounds. I've never, before or since, seen such a demonstration of sheer strength.

We loved the car, and my brothers and I kept it polished and waxed. But we knew next to nothing about maintenance. Sam asked his friend who was a mechanic what needed to be done to it, and the friend showed him how to check the oil. So every once in a while, Sam would check the oil and pour in a couple of quarts. That eased our consciences and we just drove the car.

But over time we couldn't help noticing that the Chevy was belching smoke and consuming almost as much oil as gasoline. That was when Sam decided to overhaul the engine. Of course he had no experience with this, but he did have his friend to advise him and his logic and instinct to guide him.

Sam proceeded to take the engine apart, laying the pieces all around him in the order in which they were removed. Then he changed the rings and bearings and ground the valves. He worked day and night, without eating or sleeping. But when he finished, there were no parts left over. Every piece had found its way back where it belonged.

Sam got in and put his foot on the starter, and the Chevy sprang to life. What a miracle!

About a year later, Henry decided to fix the brakes. Sam's success with the overhaul had made the whole thing seem easy. So Henry asked the mechanic how to proceed and went to work. He jacked up the rear wheel, put a block of wood under the brake housing and removed the wheel.

Then he lay down on his back and pulled himself under the car to have a look at the brakes. He attached the wrench to a nut and pulled it with a jerk. The car was so wobbly on the block that this single jerk was enough to cause it to roll forward. It landed over Henry, with the axle falling onto his chest. Almost unable to breath, he moaned a faint call for help.

My mother was in the kitchen preparing dinner. She didn't hear Henry cry out, but she did sense with a mother's intuition that something was wrong out back. She ran toward the yard, screamed at the sight of her eldest son pinned to the ground, and, sure that he was about to die, grabbed a two-by-four and shoved it under the axle. But in her anguish she found the strength to pry the car up while dragging Henry out from underneath the axle.

There's no doubt that the crushing weight would have killed

Henry in a minute or two. Her quick-action rescue saved his life. Recalling the event many years later, she said, "I never wondered if I was strong enough. I just did it."

Henry's near catastrophe left us in fear of the car. No one wanted to finish fixing the brakes. The car just sat there, rotting and rusting. I was twelve at the time, and had become inflicted with an uncontrollable need to dig holes in the ground. I wasn't searching for anything in particular, but our yard looked like an illustration for Erskine Caldwell's *God's Little Acre* where the father digs holes in search of gold. One of my holes grew to about fifteen feet in length, and I was quite proud of it.

One day my mother looked out over the carnage that had once been her backyard: craters of every conceivable size and shape and the huge hulk of a ruined car. Suddenly she had an inspiration. "Let's roll the Chevy into Carl's big hole and bury both eyesores at the same time."

It was a perfect fit. We leveled the yard, and my insatiable compulsion for digging disappeared as mysteriously as it had come.

Fifty years later, I was on a business trip to Los Angeles. On a whim, I drove out to 259 East Twenty-Third Street, the site of the burial. Most of the homes in the neighborhood were gone, and the whole area looked trashed out. Our place was a junkyard.

I found the owner drinking coffee in his office, a corrugated iron shack where our Cash and Carry Grocery had once stood. I told him about the store and about the buried car.

"Was it a '23 Chevy?" he asked.

"Yes, that's it," I replied.

"Yeah? Well, I dug it out about five years ago. Would you believe I sold it to a Chevy nut for $500. He was after the engine parts—said they were in mint condition."

THE GREAT DEPRESSION

We were by that time dealing with the vagaries of the Great Depression, and it was becoming clear that "cash only" was an excellent policy. We were fortunate to have had the store during those depression years when so many people were without work. We certainly felt the weight of poverty all around us, but we were used to getting by on little food, and the store brought in enough money to pay the lease and we always had food.

In 1929, my youngest brother Yoshito (Jim) was born. My mother had to return to work in the store as soon as possible after his birth and, as always, Yosh became the little mother for the three younger kids. She was always generous and kind to us. The next year, Chioko, Junji, and their two children joined us.

True to his superstition, Kazuichi died at the end of three years—1930. It is a sad testimonial that no member of the family wept at his funeral. Strangers, who were my father's playing friends, dominated the ceremony.

Though he didn't live to see it, all of my father's children married Japanese people just as he had wished. Why bother with logic and good sense when superstitions and dying wishes prove so accurate?

Suddenly my mother's quality of life improved, for there was no one around to batter her. She threw away the washboard and bought a washing machine with a ringer. What a luxury! Nevertheless, life was still tough, for the depression was in full swing.

STEALING, A MORTAL SIN

The third grade teacher in my Twenty-eighth Street School had a great influence on me. First of all, she found my name difficult. "I can't pronounce your name," she said, "so I'm giving you the name Carl." I've had a life-long dislike for that name. I don't feel like a Carl. But it stuck.

Still, she did something wonderful. One October day, in 1930, she took the entire class to the library to get library cards. With these amazing cards we were allowed to check out any of the books they had in the library for two weeks. This was a marvelous discovery for me.

And then I found out that we had a branch library on East Twenty-third Street—only half a block from our store.

I devoured every book in the children's book section. The series that filled me with joy were the *Doctor Doolittle* books. I read them several times.

Then I discovered the best of them all: *Chippy Chipmunk*. This children's book was written by David Cory and published in 1920. I checked it out every two weeks and read it over and over again. When I came to the last page, some irresistible force drove me back to the first page to read the story again. From a lifetime of reading, no other book has captivated me to this extent.

One day I walked over and looked up at the top shelf where the book lived when I didn't have it checked out. On an impulse, I stuck it under my shirt and, when the librarian was looking the other way, I sneaked out. I ran home and hid the book under my mattress. This felt strange to me, for normally that book would sit on a table or chair for all to see. I was filled with fear. I couldn't eat or sleep for fear of being caught and put into prison. Like Adam and Eve, I became aware that I was naked for having committed a mortal sin. After a week of agony, I had wasted away. My mother thought I must be terribly sick. She wanted me to stay home from school.

That's when I decided to redeem myself by returning the book. Once again I put the book inside my shirt and waited for the librarian to become busy with several people checking out books. I sneaked in and put the book in its rightful place.

But I never checked out that book nor did I ever read it again. The good news was that I didn't have to go to confession, for I reasoned that my last act just canceled my mortal sin of stealing.

During the past several decades, I looked for that book but have never found it. I told this story at a number of social gatherings. Friends, recalling my love of the book, searched for it and finally found several copies. I now have three. After reading the book again, I wondered why it appealed to me because Chippy was a rascal. The first chapter is an account of how Chippy was in mortal danger because Little Jack Rabbit dropped a cork down Chippy's throat. The Rabbit screamed, "And he'll swell up and bust in just a few minutes. Oh, dear, oh dear. It's all my fault." Dr. Heron came around and thrust his long beak down Chippy's throat and plucked out the cork and saved the chipmunk's life. The doctor said, "That will be five." But Chippy left the bill unpaid. Did I get the idea of stealing from the library from Chippy?

THE INVENTOR

As a child I had a passion for all things mechanical. Wheels, bolts, levers and wrenches were my friends, and I wanted to invent something. I looked around constantly for problems that needed solutions. When I was ten, a bolt of lightning struck me. I had a great invention. I attached a protractor to a level so that it pivoted about the center of the protractor. I used it for measuring the angle between the bottom and horizontal sides of stairways. I also measured roof pitches and the angles of stars.

I was proud of this invention, and figured that it had to be patented. So I answered ads I found in *Popular Mechanics*. To my horror, a patent cost between $15 and $150. One devastating bit of news compounded my money problem. While thumbing through a dictionary, I happened to notice a picture of a device that looked like my invention. A careful reading revealed that it was identical to my brainstorm. It was called an "Archimedes Level."

Since I had never heard of him, I didn't realize I was in good company or that this Greek was a famous inventor and the greatest mathematician of antiquity. Later, I learned that I was too late by twenty-three centuries. So I moved inventing onto a far back burner.

Archimedes entered my life once more when, as a graduate student, I was a teaching assistant. My job was to correct exam papers for a professor who taught physics to pre-dental, pre-medical and pre-nursing students. On the first exam, they were asked to write about the contributions of Archimedes, Galileo and Sir Isaac Newton.

One young lady wrote:

"When Archimedes, the Greek, was sitting in a bath tub, he looked down into the water and made a discovery so wonderful that he jumped out of the tub and ran down the street stark naked shouting, 'Eureka! It floats'."

We gave her an "A" for creative writing.

Nothing happened for the next thirty-five years. Then I suddenly began having a dream in which I was trying to screw a nut onto a bolt. The dream always ended before I found out if they fit.

My interpretation was that a second great invention in my subconscious was trying to break out. Progress was very slow because I dreamed only about twice a year, but I persisted for ten more years. Then I explained my dream to Dr. Olson, a psychologist.

"That's not a dream about an invention trying to bust loose," he sputtered. "It's a sexual dream of high frustration."

Dr. Olson might be right. Nonetheless I continue to be enchanted by the idea that an invention is trying to break through. Though more than sixty-eight fruitless years have slipped by, I am still poised, waiting to be struck again by that inspired "*Eureka*!"

THE DAVISES

It was in 1932 that the Davises started hawking the *Los Angeles Herald* in front of our grocery store. There were two of them. Jim, the father, was seventy-five. Like so many people during the depression, he had lost all of his teeth, and his ragged clothes hung loosely on his gaunt body. People in the neighborhood said he was an "Okie" although I never heard him say a word about his background, Oklahoma or otherwise.

Obed, his son, was twelve. He had dark hair, a winning smile and charming manners. He addressed everyone as "Sir" or "Ma'am," and was a polished businessman. It had been Obed who started the paper business. His father helped by selling papers until Obed came home from school. In fact, Obed really was the sole family income provider.

Obed was charming, but everyone really enjoyed his father. He was a colorful character who entertained his customers by doing a jig while drooling and waving a newspaper with one hand. He also told them Civil War stories.

His wife, Hettie, was only thirty-five, but they must have been hard years because she and Jim looked like contemporaries. Hettie was always cold. She enveloped her tiny body in a shawl made from a blanket she had torn in two. And she wore this shawl every day, even in the hot Los Angeles summer. Like Jim, she was toothless and, when speaking, she was hard to understand. Her graying hair never looked combed. Nevertheless, Jim was very proud of her. He was always careful to let people know that she was an Ohio woman.

Jim and Hettie's second son, Billy, was as different from Obed as night and day. Where Obed was solid and dark, Billy looked skinny and faded—his freckles were colorless, his thin, reddish-blonde hair stood high on his head and waved about like a field of grain, his mouth was always hanging open, and he rarely smiled. Obed had started the family business, but Billy never helped out. He was lazy. So lazy that he used to pee out of his second story bedroom window rather than walk down one flight of stairs. His room smelled like an outhouse, and his screen window frame was a rotting yellow.

I knew Billy the best because we were in the same grade at San Pedro Street School. But where I was a good student, Billy was barely passing. Nobody—teacher, parent—except me, ever paid any attention to him, which suited him fine. Therefore it galled me that, though I practiced the penmanship exercises, I could not get a Palmer Writing Method certificate, but Billy did! He received one even though he spelled "have" as "hove." Billy really was a marginal kid, but even so he was my friend. We had great times wrestling.

Once Billy asked me, "Do you know how to jack-off?"

"No," I replied. "What's that?"

"Let's go up to our hiding place and I'll show you."

We climbed the giant pepper tree in his yard. The tree was so huge that even at thirty feet we were able to sit and even lie down on its branches. I watched as Billy stretched out comfortably, took out his tiny penis and began to stroke it with ever increasing vigor.

Finally he collapsed from exhaustion. "I've come!" he said. "See that stuff? It's jism."

"No kidding," I said, looking at the tiny drop of glistening liquid. "It looks like piss to me."

Who would have guessed this bland blob was an exhibitionist and a sexual athlete?

Though we had tried to keep our store running on a "Cash and Carry" basis, there were creditors. It had started with one solid customer, then two, and eventually, as people were unable to find jobs, twenty-five of them. And the Davises were among them.

One evening, Jim came in and confided to my mother that they didn't earn enough from the paper business to pay us. They owed for past due rent and other expenses, so they had decided to escape in the middle of the night and go back to Ohio. My mother appreciated Jim's honesty and wrote off his debt. Then she gave him two bags of groceries to sustain them for the long drive.

The toothless man wept and thanked my mother for the only kindness he had seen since coming to California. The next morning their house was empty.

THE EARTHQUAKE

In 1933, I was climbing our back fence when suddenly the earth shook violently and threw me off. I lay on the ground and watched telephone poles waving like saplings. Some power lines broke and dropped to the ground. Maple Avenue undulated as waves a foot high rippled upward toward City Hall. This was the earthquake that leveled the city of Compton.

Inside the store, merchandise fell from the shelves. Bottles of jam, pickles and oils broke among the canned goods leaving a mess. With no electricity, the refrigerator stopped working. We had a fire sale to get rid of the perishables such as meat and dairy products. The tremors continued for a couple of days, but nobody in our neighborhood was hurt. We all kept saying things like, "Aren't we lucky to be alive?" Life returned to normal remarkably quickly and we soon forgot the earthquake.

But one ominous result of that event was the infestation of rats. They were everywhere, and it was especially bad in the store. Some that we caught in traps were about a foot long from the nose to the end of the tail. Eventually the rats became so clever that traps and poisons were useless. They ate the poisons but we never found dead bodies. Pouring water into holes with a hose for half an hour did no good at all. In the morning we continued to see their mischief. Now that I'm old and brilliant, I wonder why we didn't fill the holes with cement.

My mother became convinced that rat poison didn't kill anything. To test her opinion, she gave some to my prized black and white pet mouse. The poison was effective, for the mouse died instantly.

No apology was good enough to pacify me. "How could you do this to me?" I wailed. She carried her misdeed to her grave, for I never forgave her.

BLONDIE AND THE SEWER PIPES

A few months after the 1933 earthquake, Los Angeles County began putting in a sewer system under Maple Avenue. It was a W.P.A. project (Works Project Administration), one of FDR's attempts to put people back to work on worthwhile public works projects. This program drew many onlookers including me. I was fascinated with all the equipment, manned by workers, but the machines appeared to be doing very little work. Steam shovels dug a trench about seven feet deep and six feet wide. A crane lowered concrete pipes—five feet in diameter—into their resting places. Meanwhile, other workmen shaped the ditch with shovels so that the pipes fit properly.

Finally the ditch reached our store. It was that day that I first became aware of a young woman with blond hair piled high on her head. She arrived carrying a basket and looking like a movie star on her way to a party. Though an unusual beauty, the best thing about her was her perfectly formed legs that tapered into high heeled shoes. Wow! In an instant, at the advanced age of eleven, I became a hopeless and lifelong "leg-man."

All the workmen noticed the lady right away. They stopped working and exchanged flirtatious banter with her.

Daintily, she tiptoed to the center of the plank that forded the trench and announced, "I made cookies to sell to you. The price is ten cents."

Men scrambled over one another to get under where she stood. They jostled each other like baby birds in a nest demanding attention. They chirped, "Hey, Blondie, take my dime. I want a cookie. I'm next."

As one man bought his cookie, others shoved him aside and proffered their own dimes. I could tell that when they had worked their way underneath her, they were looking up into her loosely hung skirt. I exploded with envy.

That dime equated to about one-tenth of a day's wage for each of those WPA workers. At our grocery store, we sold one and a half pound loaves of Wonder Bread for five cents. When the bakery ran a special, we sold the second loaf for only one cent. Blondie's sales technique commanded the extortionate price of ten cents because, in addition to delivering a cookie, she played:

I see London,
I see France,

I see someone's
underpants.

I was enthralled. Each day, as soon as I got out of school, I dashed over to see Blondie's lovely legs and her show. She sold out her cookies every day. On the third day, I learned one of her sales secrets. One man, after peering up her skirt, shouted, "Hey, Blondie, how come you're not Blondie down there?"

She answered him with a smile and kept hauling in the dimes.

While the men were having a howling good time, the women who watched this spectacle clucked and hissed their disapproval with, "That hussy!" and "Those stupid men!"

I always figured that Blondie didn't slow down the work much since most of the men seemed to lean on their shovels while watching somebody else work. In fact, she may have increased the productivity by getting their hormones all charged up.

The next day was Saturday, and nobody was working. Without beauty and her show, my day was shot, so I climbed down into the ditch to look at the big pipe. Curious as always, I walked in and kept going. Suddenly I rounded a curve and everything turned dark. I panicked and started to run before I realized that I wasn't sure which way I was going. Finally I sat down to collect my senses. I visualized starving to death right there on the spot. When the County turned on the sewer, my bones would wash out to sea unnoticed, and my family would never learn what had become of me.

And then I pulled myself together and came up with a plan. I decided to walk in one direction, counting my steps, turn around and walk past my starting point, going a little farther each time. By oscillating back and forth with ever increasing excursions, I knew I'd eventually get out.

I went through several iterations of counting and turning back and, eventually, after going 450 steps, I saw a dim light ahead. I ran to it and found an opening leading to a grate on the sidewalk. Now I knew which way was out: if I kept walking with that opening on my left side, I would reach the end of the pipe. Seven hundred steps later I rounded the curve and saw the opening.

How good it felt to get out of that concrete coffin and walk on dirt again!

It was totally dark when I walked in the house. Everyone was yelling at me: "Where were you?" "We looked all over for you." "We had dinner hours ago."

I glowed as I listened to these abuses, for it was a joy to be among the living.

The next Monday, at 3:30 P.M., I was back once more to ogle my star and to listen to the men's bawdy but appreciative comments. And I continued those visits until the sewer line ended a couple of miles from home.

Blondie disappeared, and I never saw her again. But on my eyeballs, I have a permanent imprint of those gorgeous legs.

CRYSTAL SETS

Meanwhile, Jerry, the eighteen-year-old kid down the street from our grocery store had a miraculous device. The music came out of the air and into a wire. It then went to a crystal set, and music came out of the earphones. The thing was only some wire wound into a coil and a crystal with a wire spring called a cat's whisker. This whisker was adjustable so that it could touch various parts of the crystal. I probed around the crystal to find the hot spot that gave the best reception of a radio station. What a great find for an eleven year old!

Jerry wore his earphones most of the time. But he would let me listen once in a while. The upper part of his body was Mr. America because he exercised by doing strenuous feats such as one-arm chin-ups whenever he thought about them. If his legs had not been paralyzed, he would have been an awesome giant. Jerry entertained the kids in the neighborhood with feats of strength— like tearing telephone books into quarters.

I yearned for a crystal set even more than an *Erector Set* with an electric motor. One of Jerry's earphones died, so he gave me the whole headset. Now, with some wire for an aerial and a crystal set, I could listen to radio stations.

By luck, I found an old electric motor in a trash can at the service station. It was full of copper wire, but embedded with varnish. I threw the motor into a wood fire and burned out the innards so that I could take out the wires. By tying one end of the wire to a tree, I stretched it to take out the kinks. Now I had enough wires for two aerials.

Jerry tried to explain how the crystal set worked. But he used so many strange words that none of it made sense.

I urged him on. "Say it again. I'll listen more carefully."

But that did no good. It just gave me a ringing noise in my head. Finally I no longer cared how it worked. It sufficed that such a wonderful thing existed.

Popular Mechanics carried an ad for a company in Racine, Wisconsin that sold crystal sets for one dollar, postpaid. Jerry told me postpaid meant that the company paid the postage for sending me the device. I looked eastward once in a while because Racine, the city with the crystal set, was out there someplace. I called it "Raysin" until I learned years later that it was pronounced "Ray-seen."

The chances of getting a set were remote because I didn't have a cent. This was 1933, at the height of the Great Depression. My mother couldn't waste money on such foolishness. Her focus was survival. I got the job of hawking The *Los Angeles Herald* at the corner of Adams and Los Angeles Blvd. On the first day I sold three and earned three cents. On the third day, a car ran over my foot, so I had to quit. I never explained to anyone why I limped. That foot still hurts if I stand too long.

My older sister, Yosh, had $1.03, her lifetime savings, deposited at the Bank of America, but it had closed its doors in 1930.

Once, while walking home via Washington Boulevard, I noticed that the bank had come back to life. I ran home to tell Yosh. She went to the bank and retrieved her money, but with no interest. Then she gave me the dollar I needed. I was in heaven because I had a radio. What a great sister!

Though she had given me the money, recently I decided to treat it as a loan by sending her a check for $32.99 representing the $1.00 compounded at 6 percent for sixty years. Her reaction was, "What a nut! I don't recall the dollar, but I remember that crystal set. I used to listen to it once in a while."

About a year after I bought the first set, I made a coil by wrapping the spare wire from the motor around a Quaker Oats box. I used this coil in a supposedly more advanced version of a tuned crystal set. Though I didn't have the slightest idea what I was doing, I made the circuit work by connecting the components in several ways until I found a combination that worked.

A few years ago, recalling my infatuation with the crystal set, I made a good one using a modern silicon diode, variable capacitors and high performance coils. The reception was stunning. It would have been even better if I had had an old motor to burn out for its wires so that I could have had a decent aerial.

SAM

Sam, who was six years older than I, turned seventeen in 1933. I thought of him as an adult, and wasn't perturbed when he dropped out of school in his junior year to work. In 1933, we didn't spend much time thinking about the future. After all we'd been through, we all wanted to keep the family together. But we needed outside income to do that, and Sam volunteered to be the source of that income. Though our needs were urgent at the time, I wish we could have found a way for him to finish school. Sam was bright with an artistic bent, and he longed for a good education. He was the only one of the four children sent to Japan who was ever proficient in English.

Sam found a job at the Los Angeles Wholesale Produce Market where he was hired as a swamper. That meant that he spent his days moving produce around with a hand truck. He worked from midnight to noon—a twelve-hour shift. And his only day off began at 11:00 A.M. on Saturdays.

That was the most precious time of the week for me, because Sam always took me to the movies. We went to the Main Theater, near Third and North Main, which was then the sleazy part of L.A. Pawnshops, second hand stores, junk shops and vegetable stands lined the streets, and prostitutes flaunted their wares at all hours. But it was the perfect movie house for us. They never showed the same movie twice, and admission was only five cents. The first time we went, we watched all twelve chapters of Tarzan, one other serial and several other movies. After watching for ten hours, we left because we were starved.

The following week, we took a bag of fruits with us. As we ate bananas and apples we tossed the garbage under our seats. When it got too messy, we moved. Now we were able to watch from noon to midnight. Finally, conscience got the better of us. So we started taking two bags so that we could put the peelings and apple cores in a bag instead of creating a mess.

We found that most of the serials were faked. In one chapter, we would see Tarzan falling into the open jaw of a crocodile. In the next chapter, a fourth of the movie was repeated, but now Tarzan was soaring past the reptiles and landing softly on the far shore. In others, a woman with hands and feet tied struggled between railroad tracks as the train came roaring over her. Yet in the next chapter she escaped easily. We enjoyed finding fault, and had a marvelous time watching them. In that one-year we saw most of the movies that had been made in Hollywood up until then. My favorites were Ken Maynard, Hoot Gibson, Tarzan of the Apes and Laurel and Hardy.

In 1934, Sam bought a four-year-old *Indian Chief* motorcycle, the biggest cycle made by Indian Motorcycle Company. It had a two-cylinder, two-stroke cycle engine, which meant he had to mix a heavy oil, (about SAE 70), with the gasoline. Until he got protection bars, the motorcycle used to fall on him, bruising and burning his legs. He took it apart a few times to overhaul it, and that machine remained in top condition. Sam would take me with him on his motorcycle. When we roared down the highway, motorists heard us and, thinking we were the police, moved to the right to let us pass. We especially enjoyed that.

Several large, car-chasing dogs lived in our neighborhood. They especially liked motorcycles because they could reach the riders' legs and bite them. Sam decided to do something about those pests. He'd lure one to start chasing him on his right side. After the dog reached his peak speed, Sam swerved toward the curb and then suddenly turned to the left just as he approached a parked car. Seeing the car too late, the dog crashed into its rear end. It whimpered, licked its wounds and slunk home. After the second crash into a parked car, the dog decided that chasing cars hurt too much. On its third try, the dog leaped forward toward a car but, remembering the painful consequences, stopped, sat down on its haunches, and watched the car go by. Sam systematically cured every car chaser in the neighborhood, and peace reigned.

SLINGSHOTS

I loved my adventures with Sam, but I still didn't have what I wanted most. I was twelve, and I wanted a .22 caliber rifle in the worst way. But in the midst of a depression, this was a hopeless dream. The next best was a slingshot. I made several of them using carefully selected "Y's" from tree branches and rubber bands made from old inner tubes. Then I chose two bands that were equal in springiness. (I knew from experimenting that unequal rubber bands caused the shot to veer to one side.)

With practice, I became a pretty good shot, and that gave me a lot of confidence. As it turned out, I wasn't quite as good as I thought. My practice session had generally been in the backyard, where I used tin cans for targets. But on this occasion, I was in the front yard looking for new and different targets.

Then I noticed a Packard parked across the street. It was about fifty feet away, and its hood ornament was perfect. I had just taken aim at the ornament when the owner of the newly opened beer parlor walked into my line of fire. Unfortunately, I missed the ornament and hit the man.

While he was looking around to see who'd hit him, I got on my bike and rode nonchalantly toward him. He stormed into our yard and glared at me. But my innocent expression convinced him that I wasn't the culprit. He pounded on the back door and confronted my mother.

"You've got a kid in there with a slingshot," he said, "and I just got hit on the head with a rock. Where is he?"

Knowing my preoccupation with slingshots, it took only a microsecond for her to put two and two together. She walked over to the fence where I had taken refuge and nailed me.

"Carl, you did this, didn't you?"

"Yes," I replied, looking hard at my shoes.

She bonked me on the head with a stick and led me by the ear to the barkeeper. I had to confess and apologize.

The man's face softened. "Get rid of that dangerous slingshot," he said. "You were lucky you didn't hit me in the eye."

This was the first and only time my mother ever hit me, and it told me how angry she was. Slingshots became a forbidden item with her. But somehow that didn't matter much to me. I had already lost interest. Who wanted to bother with an inaccurate weapon that couldn't even hit a hood ornament?

About a year later, I came upon a picture of David slaying Goliath in a Bible. The picture was large enough so that I could see the details of David's sling. It was an oval piece of leather with thongs tied at its ends. David tied one end of the thong to his finger and the other hung loose. I visualized him placing a rock in the oval pouch and aligning the two thongs. By swinging the rock in a circular motion and letting loose of the free thong, he could toss the rock at high speed. That appealed to me a lot and of course I had to try it.

Biblical scholars might be aghast at the destructive lesson I gleaned from the Bible. Disobeying my mother, I made several. With some practice, I could fling rocks great distances and hit bottle and can targets. The throwing technique is similar to pitching a baseball except that pitchers have arms five feet long. In the overhand toss, I released the rock at the top of the swing. By swinging the rock in the opposite direction, I released the rock at the bottom for an underhand fling. I preferred the underhand shot.

The heroine of *Clan of the Cave Bear* by Jean M. Auel became an expert with the sling by developing a technique of getting two shots off. It's pretty hard to see how she did that. I certainly never managed.

A few years later, while roaming the desert in the San Fernando Valley, I came upon a covey of quails in a nest on the ground. I flung a rock and hit one. To my surprise, the others didn't fly away. I kept shooting until I had killed all six in that nest. I had become an expert with the weapon that killed Goliath, but I felt no joy.

After that success, I tossed the sling away and never hunted again. I must try looking in the Bible again for an idea I can use. Perhaps it would be something less lethal.

BANKRUPTCY

My mother closed the store in 1934. Our non-paying customers had all fallen on hard times. And, as their debts mounted, many of them, knowing they couldn't pay, quit coming to the store. Others, like the Davises, moved back home. But unlike Jim Davis, the others never came to my mother to confess. So our customer base vanished and we were bankrupt.

To keep alive, we consumed everything edible left on the shelves. Eventually, we were left with only inedible spices and soap. For some reason we hauled those spices around with us for years. It wasn't until 1940 that we finally admitted we'd never find uses for the pickling spices and the thyme and cinnamon sticks, and we tossed them all out.

It was the height of the Depression and my mother couldn't find work. My brothers had jobs, but they earned very little—

certainly not enough to support the family. Finally my mother went to talk to Shigeko's husband about our plight. Shigeko had married in 1930, when she was twenty, and they now had their own farm. He agreed to take us on as farm workers and she accepted his offer.

My mother knew she could not manage the work while taking care of five-year-old Jim. So she went to an old family friend, Mr. Nagai, who had followed our family from Montana to Los Angeles. Mr. Nagai was a sixty-year-old bachelor who peddled vegetables for a living. He agreed to take Jim to decrease our financial burden.

To this day I feel guilty for not having tried harder to talk my mother out of letting him go. I really think I could have saved him if I had spoken up on his behalf. He later told me that in Mr. Nagai's neighborhood, all the other kids had Daisy BB Guns. "I would have been happy to live with Mr. Nagai," he said, "if he had been able to get me a BB gun. But he couldn't afford it, and I was an outcast." I sent Jim a BB gun for his sixty-eighth birthday.

The farm was in Van Nuys, a farming community thirty miles north of Los Angeles in the San Fernando Valley. We lived in a tar-papered structure that had no electricity, water, sewer or windows. There were four of us living in the shed: my mother, Yosh, Ayako and me. We ate mostly what the farm produced—eggplants, green peppers, carrots, green onions, turnips. Banana squash grown by our neighbors was the greatest of delicacies. I tried some recently, but was disappointed. It tasted like squash.

All of us, including Ayako who was only eight, were expected to work sixty to seventy hours a week. Our only time off was Saturday afternoon. For this effort, my mother was paid about $1.50 a day. The rest of us worked as unpaid family workers.

I learned to cultivate with a horse, keeping at it for ten hours a day on weekends and every day during the summer. Later, when I learned to drive, I got the job of loading and unloading chicken manure. This ruined my social life because I always smelled like chicken shit.

MENTORS

Growing up as a child of the Great Depression years, I felt deeply the family's total preoccupation with survival. Where the next meal was coming from and how to pay the rent were issues of constant concern. Talk was never about possible future careers, college, politics or social problems. Everyone assumed I would become a truck driver or a farm worker, like all the other young men in the neighborhood.

Still, exploring the question of what to become when I grew up was a pleasant pastime for me. It gave me something to think about while doing mindless farm work. It turned out that whatever I was to become, depended upon the guidance of several wonderful mentors. The three who stand out in my mind are our neighbor, John Stoudt, and two teachers, Miss Wilkonson and Miss Young.

John Stoudt was a retired poultry farmer who lived on the adjoining farm. In his mid-seventies, he was hunch-backed, but still tall. And he moved around slowly. He had the habit of fussing with his pipe with his gnarled hands. I think Mr. Stoudt took time to talk to me because I was attentive to his stories even when they were repetitive. When he got excited, he swore a lot and then, when he remembered that he was talking to a fourteen-year-old kid, he would apologize.

Nevertheless, my vocabulary grew rapidly—not just with swear words, but in areas of general knowledge. Through his rambling stories, I learned about how things had been back in 1888. And, strangely enough, he opened up the world of genetics.

Mr. Stoudt was breeding a new species of silver-colored Bantam chickens. The parent of the new breed was a mutant, silver rooster, which sprang from all brown ancestors. Using the technique of line breeding, he crossed this rooster with its daughters, then again with granddaughters. After five generations of incestuous breeding, the offspring were now 31/32 silver and looked exactly like the mutant ancestor of them all. I could see the succeeding generations, separately penned, as they amassed more and more of the silver genes. This was exciting, good stuff! The next time I was in the library, I checked out a book called *You and Heredity* by Amram Scheinfeld. That clinched it: I was going to be a geneticist.

But even with that goal in mind, it still didn't occur to me that I'd have to go to college to learn the science. I had the simple notion that, when I grew up, I'd just become one.

Though I did not pursue genetics, Mr. Stoudt did inspire me to select a career. Twenty-five years later, when he would have been over one hundred, I went looking for him. His farm had been replaced by a shopping center. But silently I thanked Mr. Stoudt for his friendship and for teaching me the methods of science.

The second person that had a great influence on me was a teacher named Miss Wilkonson. I was in the ninth grade, still enchanted with Mr. Stoudt's chickens, when disaster struck at school. I was failing algebra and I didn't care.

Miss Wilkonson took me aside for counseling. She told me that I should not take geometry because that would be taking a seat away from a more deserving student. I found that embarrassing enough. But she went on to say that, since I was a person of limited abilities, I should learn to do things with my hands.

"I think," she said, "that you would do well to take both wood and auto-shops. And I will assign you to two hours of study hall. You will need the extra study time to keep up with English and Social Studies classes."

What a shock that was! My teacher thought I was stupid! How was that possible? On the other hand, since I hadn't participated in class and had done almost none of the homework, she had no reason to think otherwise.

And I had to admit that she had no way of knowing how well informed I was about poultry. "Why," I fumed, "I'll bet she doesn't even know that duck eggs take twenty-eight days to hatch."

I had to do something to regain my self-respect. The only solution was to master algebra and then excel in geometry. I had to prove that old Myrtle Wilkonson was dead wrong.

I started from page one of the algebra book, learned the principles and then solved every problem. At a junk shop, for a nickel, I bought an advanced algebra book of the 1900 vintage and mastered every page. With this massive overkill, I now knew more about algebra than anyone else in school. I enrolled in geometry and studied it with the same zeal. Having experienced the joys of excelling, I went on to bigger and better things such as trigonometry, solid geometry and Latin.

Later, I learned that Miss Wilkonson was teaching solid geometry, so I registered for her course. We never discussed my feeble mind, and she gave me an "A" without comment.

Forty years later, I located her in retirement in Sepulpa, a small town on the outskirts of Tulsa, Oklahoma. I wrote her a letter of thanks for straightening me out when I was wallowing in mud. She responded with a warm letter filled with nostalgia. She recalled that I had derived the formula for the volume of a spherical segment. Recently, while thumbing through her ancient copy of *Palmer's Solid Geometry,* a sheet of paper fell out. It was the page on which she had copied my derivation.

This caused her to wonder whatever happened to me. She said she remembered me as being a diligent student—yet another verification of John Dewey's belief that people tend to forget the bad and remember the good things.

Nevertheless, her negative counseling, unintentional or not, pointed me towards a career in mathematics and a more fulfilling life than would have been possible for me as a handler of chicken manure.

On second thought, if I had followed her advice, I would have been a partner in a trucking company and ended up rich like my older brother, Henry. But I would have missed all the fun offered by math and physics.

The third person that influenced my life was Miss Young, my trigonometry teacher. When I think of her, I remember how impressed I was as a kid when I noticed that her left arm was a stump above the elbow. Her left leg was noticeably more stout than the right one, perhaps from years of compensating for the missing arm. But as soon as she began to talk I forgot all about her arm.

This wonderful teacher challenged us with four particularly hard problems. She rewarded us five cents for each correct solution but we were sworn to secrecy lest we bankrupt her. From among generations of students, only a handful solved her legendary "Nickel Problems" and I became one of them. Those four coins, my greatest treasures, have survived a world war, a concentration camp and over thirty moves. I also remember the four problems for they are etched deeply in the hollows of my mind.

Miss Young's influence clinched it. I did major in physics with a minor in math in college and graduate school.

Later in my life, others had significant influences on my career choices, but they were refining the course set for me by Mr. Stoudt, Misses Wilkonson and Young. I am most pleased that our lives crossed as I made the transition from an embryonic blob to a person with aspirations.

ANIMAL LOVERS

Those teen years sped by, and suddenly it was November, 1940, and we were only a couple of months from our graduation from Van Nuys High School. But before we qualified for graduation, we had to complete one more requirement: a course called "Senior Problems." In the short space of only one semester, we would learn all the profound wisdom needed to face the hard, cruel world.

In our last assignment, Mrs. Ralston asked us to describe the qualities we would like to see in our prospective spouses. After thinking about it for a couple of days, I dashed off my statement, turned it in, and gave it no more thought.

The very next day, Mrs. Ralston started to read our accumulated specifications for spouses. As she went along, most students declared that interest in sex was top priority. I thought that was pretty good and wondered why I hadn't mentioned it. Then she began reading my single specification, which was, "I hope she likes animals."

My fellow students started looking around the room to try to figure out who the idiot was that wrote it. Though blood rushed to my head, I too, glanced around, faking the same incredulous look, searching for the clueless child.

Good old Mrs. Ralston didn't betray me by looking in my direction, and I was vastly relieved to escape notice.

That was such an embarrassing moment for me that it was more than forty years before I mentioned it to anyone. By that time, I had been able to convince myself that I had just been a late bloomer who hadn't known what the score was.

Recently, I was reminded of my "spouse spec" when I met Toni, a delightful woman who lives near my daughter. Toni loves all animals, including the lower forms that most of us ignore. For example, when she noticed that tadpoles had hatched in a depression in her sidewalk, she watered and fed them every day until they became frogs.

Animals reciprocate her love. When she sits on her lawn for a picnic, the ducks and chickens come looking for attention, the cat curls up on her lap, and the neighbor's one-hundred-fifty-pound mastiff leans against her and rests his giant jowls on her shoulder. It should be noted that these animals ignore everyone else.

People also respond to her. She is kind, generous and cheerful and her family adores her. A thirteen-year old girl in the neighborhood confided to my daughter that Toni is her best friend. What a testimonial!

Now that I have met my childhood ideal, and seen how people and animals relate to her, I have revised my opinion of my teenage-self and am pleased that I had the good sense to specify, "I hope she likes animals." Though a backward kid, I now know those were words of great wisdom.

But I must concede that sex was a pretty good idea too.

POMP AND CIRCUMSTANCE

The end of the school year was approaching. I looked forward to the commencement because my life up to this point was filled mostly with the drudgery of the Great Depression: monotonous poverty and mindless farm work. The days just didn't move along fast enough.

Finally, the great day arrived. I strutted around in my cap and gown. Class leaders gave their speeches and the athletes and scholars received their awards.

After we each received our certificate, Mr. Sayers began playing *Pomp and Circumstance* on the organ. I had never heard that majestic and stirring piece before, but I was sure that someone had composed it especially for our high school commencement. (It was actually written by Sir Robert Elgar in 1902 for the coronation of King Edward VII.)

At that first hearing, my spirits soared to new heights. I was enjoying what Abraham Maslow, late professor of psychology at Harvard University, called a "peak experience" in his book *Toward a Psychology of Being*. Though I have had other exciting milestones in my life, none has surpassed this one. This was such an important event in my life that I entered a bequest in my will that *Pomp and Circumstance* be played at my funeral in memory of my greatest moment.

Recently, two of my friends, independently, sent me the same *Peanuts* cartoon that described how I felt at my high school commencement. It showed Marcie and Peppermint Patty sitting side by side listening to music. Their conversation was:

Patty: "What's this piece called?"
Marcie: "*Pomp and Circumstance*, by Elgar. . ."
Patty: "I like it."
Marcie: "I do, too."
Patty: "Do you know what?"
Marcie: "What."
Patty: "I'm glad I'm alive."

Several years ago, I attended a conference on an island in Cass Lake, Minnesota. The theme of the event was "Is life fair?" As a preface to the issue at hand, each of us described our peak experience. Some talked about having the first baby, others about getting married but I recited my story about my high school commencement.

Later in the program, as a way of getting relief from the frustrating unfairness of life, we took a break by going out on the lawn. There we took turns by ten people raising one of us from a supine position to high over their heads. In total silence the lucky person was rocked several times and then lowered. In the space of a few minutes, we transformed from a state of high frustration to total calm.

Since the testimonials of this experience were so good, we had a hard time waiting for our turns. Then, I was raised and when I reached my apex, someone began humming *Pomp and Circumstance*. Thirty others joined and an operatic singer who knew the words burst into song so that even the people on the far shore, five miles away, could hear our celebration. This was a double peak experience: reliving my high school commencement and rehearsing my funeral.

The idea of playing that majestic and magnificent music at my funeral has great appeal to me because it seems both irreverent and incongruous. I can barely wait to die.

CHAPTER III

Internment

PEARL HARBOR

Van Nuys, California

By 1941, my immediate family had been living in the United States for forty-three years. My brother Henry managed to buy a truck and started his own hauling business, called "Nomura Bros. Trucking." I became one of his drivers for which I was paid five dollars a month. That was enough to support me at Los Angeles City College where the fees were only thirteen dollars a year. I worked from 5 P.M. to 1 A.M., then went to college during the day, majoring in physics. I was the only student out of 6,000 who majored in that generally detested subject.

Then, on December 7, 1941, the Japanese bombed Pearl Harbor. In disbelief, we saw our world come to an end. The *"Hate the Japs"* propaganda became intense. Our lives were a misery. *"The Enemy"* was portrayed with slant eyes, buckteeth and a sinister yellow face.

We were placed under martial law and told to stay within a five-mile-radius. In the meantime, the FBI rounded up all persons who had shown any kind of leadership abilities or who had done business with Japan. This left only the followers, women and children, to fend for themselves. Worse yet, the wives were not told why or where their husbands were imprisoned.

On January 15, 1942, the Secretary of the Navy, Frank Knox, made a hurried trip to Hawaii. While there, he made an unofficial comment: "I think the most effective fifth column work was done in Hawaii, with the possible exception of Norway."

This remark gave the American press *carte blanche* to have a field day at the expense of all Japanese-Americans. Subsequent investigations, which have been carried on for over forty years, have not revealed one instance of the fifth column activity suggested by Knox. But this didn't stop public pressure to incarcerate the *"Japs"* from mounting, as people of high influence, including Attorney General Earl Warren, later Governor and Chief Justice of the Supreme Court, voiced their fears based on hearsay.

On February 19, 1942, President Roosevelt signed Executive Order No. 9066 into law. This Order interned all people of Japanese ancestry—aliens and citizens alike. FDR did this even though the top Army and Navy Commanders believed that an invasion by Japan was highly unlikely.

This evaluation of the situation was revised to a certainty after Japan's devastating losses in the battle of Midway.

Whether needed or not, ten camps were built in barren places in California, Utah, Arizona, Idaho, Wyoming, Colorado and Arkansas. It is noteworthy that, because these camps were built in such uninhabitable wastelands, all but one remain barren to this day.

EVACUATION

Shortly after the Executive Order was signed, notices began to appear in public places. These notices said that we of Japanese ancestry must dispose of our businesses and belongings because we were going to be evacuated. Since all Japanese American leaders and other people of ability had been jailed, the rest of us floundered, trying to find ways to dispose of our belongings. Hoodlums walked through our homes and took whatever they wanted. We had the choice of selling things at one-tenth of their value or giving them away.

Some of us had a month to settle our affairs. But those who lived near military operations or aircraft facilities were given only a week. My brothers, Sam and Henry, were sure this madness would soon blow over. They packed up everything we owned and put it into storage along with the trucks and cars. Little did they know that, when they were finally allowed to return home four years later, everything would be gone.

People with the good fortune to have supportive neighbors fared much better. This country was blessed with many good people who opposed this policy of the government, the Quakers being chief among them. And some of those people took responsibility for watching over the possessions of their neighbors who had been incarcerated. In some cases, friends took care of houses, even farms, so that, when the evacuees returned home they found things almost as they had left them. These were the lucky ones who were able to pick up the threads of their normal lives.

But at the time, we were sure this was only a temporary situation; that American political leaders would soon come to their senses. So, when the appointed day arrived, we assembled, as required, in designated areas. By "we" I mean *everyone* of Japanese ancestry. This included *children* from orphanages, advanced *senior citizens* from intensive care homes, and *patients* with tuberculosis. Did someone really believe those helpless people were capable of sabotage?

The only people who were excused from evacuation were single-parent Caucasian women and their half-Japanese children. Mixed marriages were thus put under great stress because only one was required to go.

Ralph Lazo, a teenage youth of Mexican/Irish descent was so incensed by what was happening to the Japanese that he turned up on evacuation day and went to camp with his friends. Lazo was subsequently drafted and was awarded a Bronze Star for heroism in combat. Later he became a successful sociologist, but he remains a hero to us for his personal stand.

We were allowed to take only what we could carry. A few of the ten newly constructed "Relocation Centers" were ready for occupancy. Some of us were taken directly to one or the other of those centers. Those with no place to go were taken to temporary quarters. The U.S. Army took some of the evacuees to the Santa Anita and Tanforan horse racing tracks. Here, these poor people were forced to stay in horse stalls where horses had lived just hours before. There had been no attempt to clean up the dirt and manure on the floor. They stayed in those stables until their camps were ready for occupancy. Others were taken to impromptu barracks at the Los Angeles County Fairgrounds at Pomona.

My family was given only hours to leave our home. Then we went to the bus station where we were given numbered tags. We had with us only the hand baggage we could carry. Then we boarded a bus to this hell on earth they called Manzanar.

MANZANAR WAR RELOCATION CENTER

Owens Valley, California

Manzanar was constructed during a six-week period in the spring of 1942 in the barren high desert east of Mt. Whitney in the Sierra Nevada range. We were among the 10,000 people relocated there from West Coast cities. We were assigned to one room of a tar-papered barracks that had been divided into four rooms. Six of us were to live in this one room where the floor space was almost completely taken up by the cots. These cots, by the way, were World War I vintage U. S. Army.

For mattresses, the Army gave us canvas bags and told us to fill them with straw. The mess hall and latrines were located about a block apart.

Manzanar was famous for its dust storms. We ate sand and, when we woke up in the morning, the room was covered with a layer of sand.

As the reality of our situation set in, we began to wonder why we were imprisoned. We busied ourselves with made-up work, such as digging ditches, to wear ourselves out and try to stay out of trouble.

And as we worked, we struggled to understand what had happened to us. We talked about it endlessly. What had happened to the promises made by the Declaration of Independence and the protection of the Constitution? We were loyal citizens of this country, living normal lives. We had committed no crimes nor were we charged with any. We were denied the fundamental right to appear before a court and defend ourselves and protect our property.

In most societies, it is the middle-aged group who are the leaders and the doers. That generation was missing from our society because back in 1924 Congress passed an Asian exclusion act, which stopped *all* immigration of Asians to America.

As a result, we had a discontinuous population—men in their sixties and seventies, women in their forties and fifties, and teen-aged children. Only those born in this country were citizens. Most people don't realize that the *Naturalization Act of 1790* limited citizenship to only "free white persons," (and following the Civil War, the act was successfully challenged on behalf of blacks). The only non-white racial groups that were left were "Asians" and there-after, though Asians could immigrate to the U.S., all were excluded from citizenship eligibility. The Chinese were the first Asians to be excluded from immigration by a series of Chinese Exclusion Acts in 1882-1888. By 1923, an immigrant from India attempted to gain citizenship by arguing that he was Caucasian, but the Su-preme Court changed the definition of "white" to a popularly held definition and excluded him. Just to make sure that everyone un-derstood, the *Immigration Act of 1924* was passed and it expressly barred *entry* of "aliens ineligible to citizenship" from immigration, which meant Japanese and other Asians. It was not until Congress passed the *Immigrant Act of 1965* that race was finally removed as a factor.

But beginning in December of 1941 and within two months later, the FBI rounded up and jailed those Japanese leaders we did have in our community. They were mostly teachers, businessmen or journalists. We were left voiceless in America. Politically, we didn't exist since we had no one to champion our cause.

The climate of hate had provided an opportunity for special interest groups who jumped at the chance to remove us as compe-tition and at the same time acquire our land holdings. We were powerless to stop them. Only the young and the helpless were left, and we were easy to bully, round up and put away.

My mother, who was a remarkably strong woman, simply accepted her fate. She felt that, as a mere guest in this country, she had no rights. Furthermore, she wished us to do what the government wanted done.

Mizuko, my mother, didn't hate being there the way I did. She had survived thirty years of hell, always wondering where her next meal was coming from. Now her life was relatively easy, for she did not have to worry about food, rent and other living expenses. It was like a vacation for her. She taught illiterate women how to read, others how to knit and crochet. The latter were skills she had abandoned since her youth. But now she had the time for such leisure activities.

From the time of our arrival, I brooded over how to get out of this prison. At that stage of my life, I hadn't given much thought to my rights. I was one of the helpless and ignorant. I just did what I was told and was forced to waste my life in ignominy.

MIGRATORY FARM LABORERS

Rupert, Idaho

Because of the wartime labor shortage, we were encouraged to find jobs and "relocate" away from the coastline. But this was a *Catch 22* situation. We had to have a bona fide job offer from someone, a clearance from the FBI and an approval from the office of the commanding general responsible for our new area of residence. Since most of us were uneducated, unskilled and inexperienced, the prospects for a job were very slim. The paperwork took so long that employers lost interest and the offer of employment disappeared. I was trapped, so I quit trying.

I was saved from doing something stupid or dangerous by the

announcement that we could volunteer for farm work. A huge labor shortage developed in Idaho, Utah, Montana and Colorado as farmers lost their workers to the war effort.

In desperation, the farmers were turning to us for help. We, in turn, were being offered a chance to venture outside the barbed-wire fence.

The words "migratory farm laborer" conjure images of impoverished people moving from farm to farm doing menial, back-breaking work. That, and any other demeaning impression you may have about this work is probably correct. Our farm work was to be done under the supervision of armed guards. We were also told that we would return to camp when the labor shortage abated.

The people who do this work are doing so because they have no other alternative. I did have a choice, but the idea of breathing "free air" under any circumstances seemed far superior to being incarcerated. So, in 1942, at the age of nineteen, I volunteered without hesitation.

The farmers knew all about stoop labor, and they weren't about to volunteer. But ninety-one of us city folks decided to take our chances. Later, the local paper reported our mission and printed some statistics about the group. We ranged in age from nineteen to sixty, and averaged fourteen years of education. We fit a typical cross-section of society with mostly good people and a sprinkling of poor workers, troublemakers, and one who turned out to be a petty thief.

We boarded a bus in Manzanar, which took us to Rupert, Idaho, a farming community of 1,500. Rupert had a movie theater, several stores and, incredibly, fourteen churches. The founding fathers must have had huge religious differences to spawn so many churches. I think they had visions of explosive growth. Now two ghost towns, Campbell and Paul, flank Rupert.

At first we lived in tents. At 6:00 A.M. we stood in the street where farmers looked us over and then made their selections. The old and the frail were chosen last, if at all. One farmer confided that he never hired men with gloves. He reasoned that anyone concerned about getting his hands dirty could not be a good worker. The scene was reminiscent of buyers looking over a group of horses or slaves before the auction.

To avoid these daily humiliations, and to give everyone a fairer chance to work, we began contracting ourselves in groups of five or six men. For the first week or so, disagreements kept the group memberships in constant flux. But gradually stable teams were formed and the troublemakers were forced to work as loners.

I became a member of a group of six led by Taka Nishi, a young, bright and energetic worker with aspirations of becoming a writer. He was shrewd and articulate, which enabled us to get better than average contracts.

We got along well except for Aoki and Shintaku, two men in their fifties, who hated each other. They snarled and insulted each other continually, but they tolerated one another because both were hard workers and assets to the team. While Shintaku was round and very close to the ground, Aoki was just the opposite— tall, skinny, and stoop shouldered. His profile reminded me of the mummy of Ramses II now at the Cairo Museum. Shintaku had a piercing voice and he claimed proficiency on the *biwa*, a Japanese string instrument. Aoki disputed this musical skill with much scorn. He said little and, when not taking shots at Shintaku, was morose. To maintain peace, we developed the art of interposing ourselves between these enemies.

My best friend was George Murakami. Flabby and round-shouldered, George wore glasses so thick that his eyes disappeared into tiny dots. Before the war, he had attended UCLA, specializing in semantics. During off-hours, he gave me an excellent education in the English language by teaching me the etymology of many words. Though a good guy, George suffered from one terrible defect. He could not swallow water with his head tilted back from the communal jug. As a result, he always let his "slop" go back into the bottle. We'd look at his contamination with disgust and shocked disbelief. Then, in unison, we would shout, "George, you bastard, drink last."

During the eight months I worked on the sugar beet farm, I learned many things about myself and most especially about my body. Farm work is not so hard if you can remain in an upright position—reaching for fruit, pitching hay or following a cultivator. The very worst kind of farm work requires bending forward and maintaining that extended position for long periods.

If you're curious about this, here's an exercise you can try. Lean forward so that your hands dangle a few inches from the floor and hold that position for five minutes. Now imagine how you would feel if you retained that backbreaking position for an hour or even for ten hours.

I know how it feels, for that is the position you are in when thinning sugar beets with a short handled hoe.

Each day, as the hours wore on, the pain in my back got worse. Finally it became so excruciating that I couldn't think about anything else. I looked up occasionally to see how much farther I had to hoe before I could stand upright and enjoy the luxury of painlessness, then I endured the agony until I got to the end of the row. Using my left hand, I straightened the paralyzed fingers of my right hand, which had calluses that fit the exact contour of the handle of the hoe. Then, with the surge of circulating blood, the fingers would ache as they came back to life.

We would wait until everyone caught up and had a minute to flex his muscles. Then, as a team, we turned around and chopped our way down the next set of rows which vanished a quarter of a mile away. We worked strenuously to reach the end where a reward awaited us: water from gallon jugs stashed in the shade. Each, in turn, drank silently and savored every drop.

And then we moved on to the next rows. Majestic mountains in the distance remained unnoticed. Even thoughts of beautiful women didn't enter our minds. We were only conscious of pain.

We thinned sugar beets, bent into pretzels, twelve hours a day, seven days a week for two months. And as we worked, there were always the guards watching us.

Thirty years later, in Japan, I noticed many old men and women walking the streets, their backs horizontal to the ground. At first I thought this must be the result of dietary deficiencies. But later I learned that their deformities had been caused by a lifetime of farm work in a stooped position. Man's next invention after the wheel should have been something that eliminated stooping forever. Or else we should have remained quadrupedal primates.

Another thing I learned during this period was that the body has an amazing capacity for enduring pain. Through sheer will, we can force it to withstand pain in ever increasing amounts. There is a limit, of course, but I never reached it.

Why do people in their right minds keep on going when they are in such miserable pain? In my case, I was committed to doing my share as one of six members of a work crew. But I'm still not sure why we worked so hard. Surely, we could have worked at a more leisurely pace. In the end, working slower just wasn't practical because working hard netted us only a dollar-fifty per day after paying room and board expenses.

Finally the thinning season ended and the weeding began. What luxury! This process involved standing upright and using long-handled hoes. It was child's play, for there was no pain. We daydreamed, talked, and some even sang. Life as a lowly migratory farm laborer no longer seemed that bad. As the season progressed, we topped sugar beets, pitched hay and stacked bales, picked potatoes or threshed grain. Some of the work was dirty, but our backs didn't hurt. We were in migratory heaven.

Though still under guard, our living conditions improved when we moved into an abandoned Conservation Corps (CC) Camp. Spared the stooped labor, the men now had enough energy to socialize. The favorite games were craps and poker.

I liked poker better because it involved both luck and cunning. Old man Nishida was the pro of the bunch. He may have been no more than sixty but he looked ancient. His right eye was watery—the result of having been speared with a pitchfork in a haying accident. His body language sent the constant message, "Don't fool with me kid, you'll lose." When dealt aces up, he'd look at his hole card and, with no comment, would sometimes lay out a twenty-dollar bill. Remember, that twenty dollars represented thirteen days of work. The old man's timing and reading of his opponents were almost perfect, for those who called, paid dearly.

I never played, but I watched every night and tried to guess what each player was thinking and how Nishida decided what to do. I spent most of my time trying to get into Nishida's head. From these observations, I learned that poker was not a card game, but one of psychology, where you had to figure the odds and manage your money.

The most dreadful moment of the eight months I spent working on the sugar beets was caused by emotional, not physical pain. It happened on the day we saw German prisoners of war working in sugar beet fields. We learned to our chagrin that their conditions were better than ours were, and, further, that they received better pay and free clothes. It was hard to contain the anger that gnawed at our guts.

SLEEPING ON POTATOES

Twin Falls, Idaho

When winter came, most of the men chose to go back to Manzanar. But my coworkers wanted to continue working through the winter sorting and sacking potatoes. I stayed because I was not ready for imprisonment again. Besides, Shintaku and Aoki had finally stopped fighting after exhausting every possible way of insulting each other.

The root cellar was cavernous and it reeked of rotting potatoes. After only one day, we got used to the odor and never noticed it again. Indeed, fresh air now had a funny smell. We lived like moles, working in a dimly lit hole during the day and coming out only at night.

Though there was no noticeable difference between the dark of night and day, being creatures of habit, we still toiled during the normal working hours and slept at night. By wriggling around, I formed a contour bed and slept on top of the potatoes.

Since we had an infinite supply of potatoes, we ate them three times a day and never got tired of them. Evidently, those roots had all the nutrients needed because nobody suffered from scurvy or other horrible disease. I wonder where we got our vitamin D since we never drank milk nor saw the sun. The only minor health problem occurred when Jack, our introvert, came back from a visit to Burley with an infestation of "crabs," *Pediculus Homanus.*

Although we worked with dirty potatoes all day long, at night we became sparkling clean by bathing in an irrigation canal nearby. This became an ingrained ritual so even when ice formed, we still bathed in the canal. Once, when the ice was an eighth of an inch thick, during a moment of insanity I did a flat dive to smash the ice. At the bottom of the ditch I scraped barbed wire and slashed myself from face to toe.

I sank to the bottom and felt nothing. But when I came out, I was red with oozing blood. My colleagues almost passed out. Luckily I had missed my eyes and other vital parts. And I lived. What foolishness!

When we had finished sorting and sacking every potato in the root cellar, we disbanded. I had five dollars, the exact amount I started with, plus a newly acquired, used clarinet.

MINIDOKA RELOCATION CENTER

Jerome, Idaho

The others returned to Manzanar, but Jack and I decided to visit Minidoka, an internment camp not far from where we were.

We checked in with the expectation of being able to return to Manzanar. Instead, we became internees of Minidoka with no hope of leaving. Our only avenue of escape was through the impossible process of relocation. We were stuck in that muddy and unfriendly prison of total strangers.

Four months later, a social worker heard about my plight and arranged to transfer me to Manzanar. An armed guard escorted me on the bus trip. He always sat on my right so that his gun pointed at me as though I were a dangerous convict. He even stood behind me at the urinal. He talked to me only when he had to give me instructions such as, "Go to the left." When we stopped in Reno, I saw soldiers in brand new army woolen uniforms with patches that said "Italy." They wandered about freely, and some were playing the slot machines. These free agents were Italian prisoners of war, and we were still at war with Italy. Why were soldiers of the enemy free while, I, a citizen, wore rags and was guarded by a government agent with a gun pointed at me?

The message from the government of the country I thought was mine now became clear: "We distrust your loyalty and consider you less worthy than prisoners of war from Italy and from Germany."

This was the lowest point in my life. I looked up from the bottom of the pit and saw my life's mission. I must climb out of that hole and prepare myself to oppose people in powerful positions or influence from disenfranchising innocent American citizens. This required two things: an education to show me what to do, and enough achievements so that people would respond to me.

Was all that work as a migratory worker worth the free air I breathed? Yes, it was. I learned about the miserable lives of the migratory workers; that we can endure great pain by sheer will; and the effectiveness of teamwork. The poker strategies I learned from Mr. Nishida have given me enjoyment for almost sixty years. I regret that my "free air" time was cut off by the unintended internment at Minidoka, and that I had to see how well our POW's were treated compared to us.

RELOCATION AND A NEW JOB

Chicago, Illinois

When I returned to Manzanar, I discovered there was a program for recruiting us to serve in a segregated infantry unit. I decided against enlisting because I didn't like the reason the recruiting officer gave us: "You should volunteer to prove that you were not a traitor to the United States."

After this insult, I was more than ever determined to find a way out of the camp. But it still was impossible to find a relocation job.

Then the United Church of the Brethren in Chicago came to my rescue. They offered to sponsor me and allow me to live in their seminary dorms while I looked for a job and a place to live.

The United States Government gave me a one-way ticket to Chicago and twenty-five dollars. I found a job working as a receiving clerk, moving 550-pound barrels of chemicals and 200-pound bags of sand. I rented a room, but by then I had only two dollars left until payday, one week hence. Since I needed money for the streetcar, I had little left for food. I bought a single box of Saltine crackers. Those crackers and water kept me alive for a week. Saltine crackers are still manna for me. Years later, a woman who heard me tell the story sent me a gift-wrapped box of Saltine crackers.

As the war came to a close in 1945, the camps were closed. The elderly and the helpless were the last to leave. The most tragic were the old people who were given only twenty-five dollars and returned to the corner where they had been picked up four years before. The lucky ones had children to help them. But the childless were in desperate straits. What happened to them?

After more than thirty years of discussions, the leadership of the Japanese American Citizens' League (JACL) decided that a redress consisting of a formal apology accompanied by a cash award were the only ways of preventing recurrences of tragedies of this type.

Eventually, the government formed a committee of officials and private citizens to hear testimony and then to make recommendations. The recommendations of this committee were in accord with the suggestions made by JACL, namely an apology and a cash award. The House of Representatives approved a redress in the form of HR 442 by a two to one majority. The Senate approved their accompanying bill S1009 by sixty-nine to twenty-seven.

President Reagan signed the Redress Bill on August 10, 1988. All former internees who were alive on that day received an award of $20,000. Public reaction varied, with comments such as:

> "Why spend money when we have such a big deficit problem?"
>
> "They deserve it. Pay."
>
> "Why should the present generation pay for the sins of earlier ones?"
>
> "If we pay this one, we will open the floodgates for the Indians, Blacks and others whose rights have been violated."
>
> "Why can't we let bygones be bygones?"

My personal reaction was that I felt somewhat embarrassed receiving money from my country at a time of financial crisis. But I do agree, unless sufficient force is applied, this kind of disaster could easily happen again. Consider the liberties taken by our leaders. At this writing, and in response to the September 11, 2001 attack on the New York World Trade Center, there are at least two known U.S. citizens being held by the Justice Department *indefinitely*, without access to lawyers and without being charged with any crime on the grounds the U.S. President has declared them "enemy combatants." In addition innocent Arab Americans are being racially profiled and several have been shot in hate crimes. Two Civil Service Commission appointees of President George

Bush have openly stated that should another attack like September 11th occur, *all* Arab Americans will be rounded up and placed in "relocation camps."

The Declaration of Independence guarantees us "life, liberty and the pursuit of happiness." During W.W.II, Japanese Americans were given life, but denied the other two. The law of the land used to be that you were innocent until proven guilty. In our case, we were declared guilty without a supportable charge.

Unless it is acknowledged that mistakes were made, the stirring statements found in the *Pledge of Allegiance* and the *Declaration of Independence* will mean nothing more than "flag waving" and "Fourth of July rhetoric."

If I had known about Henry David Thoreau and Leo Tolstoy and their teachings of civil disobedience for unjust laws, or of Mahatma Gandhi and his non-violent resistance to force, or of the more recent accomplishments of Martin Luther King, Jr., I would not have gone to Manzanar but would have chosen, instead, to go to jail.

RETURN TO MANZANAR

Owens Valley, California

In 1985, I visited the remains of Manzanar, a wasteland south of Lone Pine, California. I stepped out of the car into a howling wind almost strong enough to force me back into the car. The dust was so thick I couldn't see my hand in front of me.

I was near the place where the entrance used to be, and I saw a plaque. Holding a Kleenex over my nose and mouth, I ventured toward it and read this statement:

> "In the early part of WWII, 110,000 persons of
> Japanese ancestry were interned in relocation cen-
> ters by Executive Order No. 9066, issued Febru-
> ary 19, 1942. Manzanar was the first of ten such
> concentration camps. It was bounded by barbed
> wire and guard towers, confining 10,000 persons,
> the majority being American citizens. May the
> injustices and humiliation suffered here as a re-
> sult of hysteria, racism and economic exploitation
> never emerge again."
>
> California Registered Historical Landmark No.
> 850.

The Japanese-Hawaiians, living 2,500 miles closer to the enemy,
were spared. Oddly, the government ruled that they not be interned for the same reason the mainlanders were imprisoned,
namely, military necessity. The Hawaiian-Japanese were needed
for the war effort.

During the next four decades, I pondered these questions:

> Who are we?
> Why were we put away?
> What happened to us afterwards?
> Was it necessary?
> Can it happen again?

Most people agree that it was not justified, but a few still believe that our then-president, Franklin Delano Roosevelt, and the
government were infallible. For example, at a symposium where I
was a speaker, a man in the back row set out to prove that I was

wrong in my claims of injustices. His line of questioning was:

"Did they shoot you?"

I answered, "A deranged man was shot for wandering beyond the barbed wires. But no, we were not shot."

"Weren't you lucky! Look at what atrocities you committed to our boys. Did they gas you?"

"No, we weren't put in gas chambers."

"Weren't you lucky! Look at what the Germans did to the Jews. Surely you suffered no permanent psychological damages."

My wife answered, "The damages were so great that my mother committed suicide."

He stopped interrogating, but I'm sure he still believed that the evacuation was justified.

If I had been an alien being interned during the war, it would not have been an issue. But the interrogator cited above could not acknowledge that I am an American citizen, born in Montana, and that I have the same rights as he. Five generations of my family have lived in the U.S. for more than a century—probably longer than my interrogator's family. Still he felt free to assume that I was a citizen of the enemy country.

This is a frequent misconception held even by well-educated, well-informed people. For example, while I was an executive at Honeywell, Inc., I was taking a-half-dozen customers to a fancy Minneapolis restaurant called the White House. I arrived a little early and was waiting outside for the others when I noticed a lady with a flat tire nearby. She was looking helplessly into the trunk, so I offered to assist her.

"You can't," she moaned. "There's no spare tire back here."

"It's under the trunk floor. I got to the restaurant a little early, so I have time to change it if you like."

"Thank you," she said. "That would be wonderful."

While I worked, she chatted with me.

"I'm a high school teacher, and I'm returning from a teachers' conference."

Then she asked me a series of questions.

"Where did you come from?"

"California," I replied.

"And where did you learn to speak English so well?"

"I was born here."

"Oh," she replied. "And which restaurant is it that you work in?"

I thought this well-educated woman should know better than to ask me such an annoying stereotypical question, so, with tongue in cheek, I replied, "Why I work at the White House Restaurant, right there."

"You have been so kind. Please let me give you a dollar."

"No, that's all right. The restaurant pays me very well."

I wrote a poem once to commemorate the farm worker's plight. It's in the French villanelle form.[1]

THE MIGRATORY FARM WORKER

I hoe and hoe—the end is not in sight.
My back complains; the pain depletes my mind.
A whack, a whack, a thousand more with might.

The weeds must go; the beets must stay a 'right.
The sweat now runs in sheets and makes me blind.
I hoe and hoe—the end is not in sight.

My body begs to stop, but still I fight.
From whence it comes? The will! The heart? The mind?
A whack, a whack, a thousand more with might.

I must be sure I earn enough by night.
For food, the basic need of mankind.
I hoe and hoe—the end is not in sight.

No rest, no lovely thought for my delight.
I search in vain for work I'm more inclined.
A whack, a whack, a thousand more with might.

The migratory life entraps despite
My wish to leave this hopeless grind.
I hoe and hoe—the end is not in sight,
A whack, a whack, a thousand more with might.

CHAPTER IV

The United States Army

UNIVERSITY OF MINNESOTA

Minneapolis, Minnesota

After being relocated from Manzanar to Chicago, I worked hard and saved enough money to go back to college. I applied to twenty universities around the country and was rejected by most of them. My grades were excellent, but obviously I was still considered a security risk.

The University of Minnesota and the City College of New York were the only schools challenging the trend. The University of Minnesota had already enrolled hundreds of Japanese Americans when I began my classes in the fall of 1944. I received a wonderful acceptance letter from the admissions officer who welcomed me with open arms. Not only that, they also approved my request to be treated as a resident of Minnesota since I was barred from living in my home state of California. It was wonderful being back in school.

My roommate's name was Rod. Though only a ninety pounder,

he claimed Hawaiian ancestry. I had always thought they were gargantuan people. True to his heritage, he preferred to squat. When he studied, he squatted on his chair and chain-smoked. He kept an ashtray on his desk, a foot in diameter, almost always filled with butts. When his funds ran low, he rewrapped three butts to make one full-length cigarette. He gave up only when nothing salvageable remained. One of his favorite jokes on his friends was to offer his ashtray and ask, "Hey, you want a smoke?"

We lived like paupers in a room with two desks, two chairs, two single beds and a naked light bulb that hung between our desks. We had four mattresses, but all had big holes in them. For a while, we curled around those holes until we realized that we could stack mattresses two deep and fill the holes with rags. Though crummy, the price was right. We paid only ten dollars a month rent.

Before falling asleep, Rod had to have his last smoke while lying in bed. He would put his ashtray, filled with butts, right next to his bed so that he could flick in his ashes. I don't know why he bothered, because he missed that big target most of the time. Then, in the morning, he'd step on one edge of the ashtray, flip it over, and dump his ashes on the floor. He repeated this ritual seven mornings a week.

But that didn't matter to me. I was euphoric. It was heaven to be back in my beloved math and physics classes, listening to professors who were on the cutting edge of technology. It was like starting life all over again.

My euphoria was short-lived. It was only a few weeks later that I was called in for an interview at my local draft board where they informed me that my classification had been changed from 4C to 1A.

"What's 4C?" I asked the draft board clerk.

"*Enemy alien*, ineligible for military service."

Evidently I had lost my citizenship and then recovered it by becoming 1A.

I checked out of college and gave all my belongings to Rod. The night before induction day, I attended a dance at the Wesley Foundation of the University Methodist Church. And that is where I met Louise Takeda.

She danced light as a feather while I wheeled her around the dance floor as though I were pushing a hand-truck. Then I walked home on air before realizing that I didn't know her name or address. Because of that stupidity, I figured I wouldn't be able to contact her while I was in the army.

Later that same night, I took Rod to the White Castle Hamburger shop. My total cash assets were fifteen cents and a streetcar token. Since my friend was penniless, we shared a hamburger and each had a cup of coffee.

I wished him luck with his last class. When Rod first became my roommate, he had been going to college for seven years and had amassed a total of 177 quarter credits. He needed only three more credits and a grade of at least a "D," to graduate from the College of Liberal Arts. To wrap up, he signed up for a three-credit course in physical chemistry. He wrote me later that he had gotten an "F." Then he couldn't graduate unless he earned at least three credits of "C" in something. "I can't do it," he wrote. "To hell with it."

Rod went to a trade school to learn cooking and baking. He graduated and returned to Hawaii where he became a baker.

After this wild spending spree, I, too, was penniless. In the morning, I took the Como-Snelling streetcar to Ft. Snelling where I became a U.S. Army inductee. After being sworn in as #37786556, I stood and waited. The other new recruits were called out one by one. Finally I was the only one left in the room. A Private First Class (PFC) came up to me and said, "We didn't know what the hell to do with you, so we put you in the Army Reserves. Go home and let us know your address. When we need you, we'll call you."

"But I have no home," I replied. "My mother is incarcerated at Manzanar, a relocation center. I've checked out of school and I moved out of my room. I don't have a cent. All I have is this clarinet and a toothbrush."

He took me to the USO building where a kindly, gray-haired lady listened to my plight and then gave me a cup of coffee, a donut and a street-car token, which at that time cost six for a quarter. I went to downtown Minneapolis and tried to figure out what to do.

When I passed a pawnshop, I formulated a plan: hock the clarinet, buy a Greyhound Bus ticket to Manzanar, and stay there until the Army called me. Brilliant!

But, alas, the clarinet did not yield enough money for a ticket to California. So I bought a ticket to Amache, Colorado where my older sister, Shigeko, was interned. Luckily, she had enough money to get me to Manzanar.

MANZANAR RELOCATION CENTER

Owens Valley, California

I moved into barracks No. 15-6-1 with my mother and two siblings and waited for the call to arms. I learned to play Pinochle, and I kept at it day and night. What a klutz! I should have been chasing girls. But what is a late bloomer to do?

Finally, after four months of idleness, I received my papers from the Army, a meal ticket, and authorization for a bus ticket from Lone Pine, California to Ft. Douglas, Utah.

The mess hall people packed me a lunch and, after saying good-bye to my friends and family, I had the guards at the Manzanar entrance drive me to the bus stop in Lone Pine.

As I waited, a lady not more than five feet tall stood high in front of me, spat into my face and shouted, "Take that, you dirty Jap, for what you are doing to our boys in the war."

I wiped away her spittle and backed away. What bigotry! I could have snuffed her out with one blow. She was confident of the support she would receive from the other waiting passengers and was sure that she was being patriotic by persecuting me. I don't think it occurred to her that I might be one of those boys, on her side, going off to war to be shot up.

BUCK PRIVATE

Fort Douglas, Utah
Camp Hood, Texas

At Ft. Douglas, I threw away my clothes and donned an army uniform that didn't fit. When the orders came out, the other men left. Just as it happened at Ft. Snelling, a PFC kitchen-police-pusher came to get me and said, "Hey, they don't know what to do with you. So, for the time being, you are assigned to permanent KP. Report to the kitchen at 4 A.M. I'll tell you what to do."

Wave after wave of men came to the Fort and left for basic training while I manned the dishwasher and scrubbed scorched pots and pans.

After several weeks of kitchen duty, the Army shipped me to

Camp Hood, Texas for basic training. I was in the barracks with several men who said they just graduated from Marblehead. I thought they had received advanced training, but it turned out that they were illiterates who had been taught to read and write. One recruit from Arkansas was so pleased with his newfound skill that he wrote letters every day. I wondered who would read them, but I never asked.

Though basic training was a harsh life, the Marblehead graduates still had enough energy left to shoot dice. These games were not brisk because they took a lot of time arguing about how many spots were to be counted at each throw.

THE ARMY SPECIALIZED TRAINING
PROGRAM (ASTP)

Philadelphia, Pennsylvania

After we graduated, the lieutenant called us in to tell us about our assignments. They gave me three choices. The first was to go to OCS (Officers' Candidate School), which I declined since the war had come to an end in Europe. The second was to study Serbo-Croatian. I declined this one also. But I agreed to the one that called for studying Japanese at the University of Pennsylvania.

There were about one hundred men in the ASTP (Army Specialized Training Program). We were men with high Army test scores—bright men, but we did have some trouble marching correctly. Many were embarrassed to be in this unit because they were studying while their comrades were perishing in the real war.

Someone began singing a song while we marched to the tune of "My Bonnie:"

> Oh take down your flag, mother,
> Your son's in the ASTP
> Oh take down your flag, mother,
> Your son's in the ASTP.
> A
> S
> T
> P
> Your son's in the ASTP. TP.
> A—S—T—P—
> Your son's in the ASTP.

Everyone sang, so the guilty sentiment must have been strong.

The Southerners in the unit fought the Civil War again with the Northerners. It turned out that half of the men were Jewish, so there were many discussions about why the Jews were so much smarter. Was it heredity or the culture? Warshawski offered the theory that the smartest were the Polish Jews because they had survived seven hundred years of persecution. All the dummies had been bred out. (I heard this theory again, fifty years later in Port Townsend, Washington.)

Suddenly, after a month, disaster struck. I missed a class and missed a test. There was no option for makeup. I was a "wash-out."

THE POKER LOUNGE

Fort Bragg, North Carolina

The Army transferred several of us failures to Fort Bragg, N.C., the home of the famed paratroopers.

By the time I arrived in North Carolina, Japan had surrendered and World War II was over. The Armed Services began discharging the servicemen, and the work that remained was mostly in scaling down. I was attached/unassigned, which meant I had no job. A corporal told me to find an empty barracks and stow my gear, then to go to a certain building to pick up my pay. It totaled twelve dollars and forty cents after the many deductions.

While stationed at Ft. Bragg, I shared a room with a Tech Sergeant, a thirty-year man who had the job of inspecting the mess halls at the Eastern Seaboard Army Facilities. Since he traveled during the week and went home on weekends, I had the room to myself most of the time. Several of us started playing poker after work on fridays. The games kept going longer and longer until finally they were continuing around the clock and ending early Monday morning. My room became the poker lounge because all of the others out-ranked me. In addition, I had the biggest room due to the perks of my high-ranking NCO (Non-Commissioned Officer) "roomie."

As the game progressed, the smokers flicked their cigarette butts against one blank wall. Most of them extinguished on impact, but a few smoldered away on the floor. Some of the more fastidious players would venture over to the wall once in a while and stamp out the live butts. By Sunday night, a mound of hundreds of butts had formed at the foot of the "butting" wall.

I inherited the job of sweeping up the mess. This disgusted me, because I didn't smoke, even at my advanced age of twenty-three.

One Sunday night, after everyone had left, I found an almost full pack of "Luckies." On a whim, I smoked one. I choked and wheezed, but I learned to smoke. By noon the next day, I had finished the pack. I replenished my stock by buying a whole carton of Lucky Strikes for a $1.25 at the PX. "What a bargain," I told myself. "That's so cheap, I can't afford not to smoke!"

After several months of waiting, they enrolled me in a steno school to learn typing and Gregg shorthand (the 1927 vintage).

THE KISS

Los Angeles, California

Nothing was happening and I was bored. Not just bored, but lonely. I'd never been very good with girls and it was starting to eat at me. I thought about Louise every day, but had no way to contact her. And she'd probably forgotten all about me. What a lousy life! And then I'd think, why was I making such a big deal over a crummy kiss? It was only flesh against flesh. And who could I kiss, anyway? I agonized over this. Mary was the only girl I really knew, but I hadn't seen her for years. Finally I decided, what the hell. I'd write to her and suggest we get together.

To my amazement, she answered my letter with an invitation to visit her over New Year's. "I'm house-sitting and I'll be alone," she wrote.

I squandered my jealously hoarded furlough time, three month's pay and a six thousand-mile round trip for a possible first kiss. What a triumph for biology and the morale of the troops!

While we danced I admired her curves and marveled at how soft she was. What a transformation from that knobby-kneed eleven-year-old I knew who could climb trees and knock baseballs out of the field.

We kissed, but no cannons went off in my head. How come? "Open your mouth a little and relax," she coached.

This triggered Hank's advice: "Keep your eyes open to see what effect you are producing."

I should have listened because my aim went wild. Instead of meeting softness, my teeth smashed into hers. A disaster! I regained composure and kissed her like Clark Gable kissed Vivian Leigh.

What's this? She *had* eased her tongue into my mouth. This must be a French kiss? "Big Bertha" blasted off in my head. The kiss was warm and wet and delicious. Who needed heaven; I was there. Thanks to Mary, I no longer cared if I were shot. I had tasted life at its best.

THE MORTUARY DETAIL

Governor's Island, New York

Upon graduation from steno school, I was assigned to the mortuary section of the First Army at Governor's Island off the coast of New York City.

This may have been the most top-heavy chicken outfit in the Army, for in that small installation there were thirteen General Officers, one hundred five Bird Colonels, one hundred ten First and Master Sergeants, and five Privates. I was one of the lowly ones. We outranked only the POW's who policed the island.

I was a stenographer in a clerical pool, presumably attached to a Lieutenant Colonel. A civilian by the name of Kilroy was in charge of my labor pool. He always looked very busy and harried, but he never called me for work.

I sat in the back of the room with a typewriter in front of me. It was one of those early electric models that jammed all of the keys if you happened to touch two at the same time.

A month passed and I received no stenographic assignment, so I began taking correspondence courses from various universities. One day, while I was working on an assignment in a course in vector analysis, the Colonel came around and looked over my shoulder.

"What's a vector?" he asked.

"Sir, a vector is a mathematical quantity that has both magnitude and direction."

"Oh," he said, disappearing into his office.

About a week later, the Lieutenant Colonel called me in to take dictation. I wrote down the address and waited for him to go on. He dictated, "Request granted."

I dashed it off in shorthand, typed the letter and put it on the desk for his signature. That was the sum total of my application of my training in typing and shorthand.

DISCHARGE

Van Nuys, California

The Army discharged me as a PFC in October of 1946. I rose to this lofty rank because a law was passed that required all privates to be promoted to PFC after eighteen months of service. I returned to the University of Minnesota, Institute of Technology, on the G.I. Bill of Rights.

I re-entered the University as a physics major, math minor, and studied hard. I rented a room in a private residence, and made friends with Bob Siem, the undergraduate living next door. His eight-foot-square room was even smaller than mine, and unheated, and he was sleeping on what looked like a cedar chest. I invited him to move in with me—I had an extra twin bed—and we became fast friends. We worked together at Pioneer Hall, washing dishes and mopping floors in exchange for meals.

Everything seemed to be working out for me. But every day, as I walked through campus, I continued to look for Louise, the light-as-a-feather girl I had danced with the night before my induction.

Then, after searching fruitlessly for two months, I spotted her walking down the street. Overjoyed, I rushed up to her. "Hello!" I said.

Her response was unpromising. "And who are you?"

She had only a dim recollection of our encounter, but agreed to have coffee with me. I told her I'd been looking for her every day. She laughed. "I'm a student nurse and I've been working nights," she said. "I've been sleeping while you were roaming the campus."

What a one-sided affair this had been. I'd thought about her every day while I was in the Army! My studies suffered while I corrected this problem.

In December, I wrote to Mary in California to tell her I was going to marry Louise.

She wrote back immediately. "Don't do it! We could have a good life. Come see me so that I can talk you out of it," she wrote.

I married Lou December 23, 1947.

CHAPTER V

Louise Takeda

HER FAMILY

San Francisco, California

Before the turn of the century, a young man named Yonekichi Takeda immigrated to California. Eight years later, his family arranged for a bride for him. Her name was Sumiko Nakagawa. It was a happy marriage, but the couple had difficulty conceiving a child. Finally, in 1916 they were blessed with a daughter. But she died during the influenza epidemic of 1918. You can imagine their joy when Louise was born in 1923. They gave her the name Louise in honor of the attending nurse at San Francisco General Hospital.

In the next three years, three more siblings were born. The parents wanted their children's names to rhyme when mispronounced in Japanese. Since Louise became Ru'ee'su when mispronounced, the second daughter was named Grace, which became Gu-ray-su. Peter's name became Pee-ta, and Elmer's name was Eh-ru-ma. Of course, they rhymed!

Louise grew up a veritable princess, with her loving father providing her with every need. Once, when the parents were fretting about what would happen to their children if they should die, Louise said, "Don't worry. We have that one hundred pound sack of rice in the back room. We will live on that."

When Louise was nine, her mother knew she was going blind. Sumiko suffered both from glaucoma and cataract ailments that could not be treated in 1935. She taught Louise to read Japanese in the hope that her daughter would be able to read to her from the Japanese literature she loved so dearly. She taught her by having her write the Chinese characters on her hands.

Eventually, Louise was able to read to her mother, and she continued working on her Japanese long enough to become fluent. When we visited Japan years later, her skills were very useful.

SCHOOL YEARS

Walnut Grove, California

Louise's spunk was evident at an early age. Her family, and later her teachers, understood her leadership abilities, and early on she became a fearless fighter for the underdog.

Her first big battle with authority came in junior high school. Back in the 1930's, the town of Walnut Grove, California had two schools: one called "White," the other, "Oriental." The "Oriental" school included children of Chinese, Japanese, Korean, Filipino and, oddly, students of Mexican ancestry. Clearly this was a segregated school for the "undesirables."

Louise was angry because the "Oriental" school students had

to write on paper that had already been used on one side by the students in the "White" school. She also resented their used and outdated sports equipment, all hand-me-downs from the privileged "White" school. But the used paper was particularly infuriating because Louise was a natural born artist. She had always loved to draw and, from childhood, made little sketches to fill every idle moment. Used paper didn't work for her delicate sketches and she saw no reason why she shouldn't have fresh paper to use. And, in the more global sense so typical of her, she was furious that the "Oriental" school students were getting second-class treatment.

In 1936, when Louise was an eighth grader, her anger moved her to action, and she organized a strike. The students knew that the Principal, Miss Woods—(Louise nicknamed her Miss Woodpecker)—was the one who had imposed the unequal treatment in their school. So Louise convinced all the students to stomp out of class *en masse* while chewing gum noisily in defiance of the school rules and chanting, "Down with Miss Woodpecker. Down with Miss Woodpecker."

The rebellious students then assembled under the railway trestle and signed Louise's petition stating their complaints about the injustices. Louise signed herself as "Ginger Rogers." Others used "Shirley Temple," "Tom Mix," and "Mickey Mouse."

On the following morning, the headline on the front page of the local paper, *The Sacramento Bee*, read:

WALNUT GROVE ORIENTAL SCHOOL
STRIKES FOR FIVE MINUTES

The article described the shortage of equipment, the out-dated books and used paper and pencils the students were required to use. After that, Louise's school was supplied with clean paper and new sports equipment.

I would like to report that Louise's zest for justice didn't stop there. Forty years later, in 1976, a peace group conducted a march in front of the general offices of Honeywell, Inc. The group's protest of Honeywell's continuing participation in military contracts was directed against management. And, as a representative of management, I stood accused. A group of us on the top floor of headquarters had gathered at the window to observe the demonstration.

A colleague standing next to me said, "Isn't that Louise down there?"

I spotted her in the front row. She was carrying a large placard. "Yes," I replied. "There she goes again, enhancing my career."

I have to add that, only a few years later, Honeywell did drop out of the military business.

Louise had a wonderful childhood, but in 1941, when she was eighteen, her family suffered three major disasters. First, her eleven-year-old younger brother died from an overdose of anesthesia during a minor operation. Two months later, before they had recovered from the shock of his death, her surviving brother and sister, driving home from a movie in the family truck, were hit by a car and forced into the river. The driver didn't even stay to see if he could help them, and both children died in the accident. The family was devastated.

And then came Pearl Harbor and the start of U.S. involvement in World War II. Louise's family, like all those of Japanese lineage in the western part of the United States, was sent to a relocation center. The Takedas were imprisoned at the Gila River Internment Camp in Arizona. Like the Nomuras, the Takedas lost their business, their personal possessions, and their civil rights.

It was an incredibly difficult situation, for her mother was blind. But Louise made the best of it by being socially active in camp and enjoying the task of teaching a fifth grade class.

And she found a way out. In 1943 she was twenty, old enough to apply for the relocation program. This program existed because of the acute labor shortage that hit this country after the war started. Louise was able to get a job as a house-girl in Minneapolis.

Though she had no money, she soon realized that she could get a college education by joining the Cadet Nurse Corp. In 1944, when she joined up, her mother chastised her. "Why become a nurse? Be a doctor." But that wasn't possible. The University Medical School placed quotas not only on women entrants, but also on Asians. Louise knew she'd never get in with both strikes against her.

CHAPTER VI

Marriage

THE WEDDING

Minneapolis, Minnesota

When I proposed marriage to Louise, she didn't immediately jump at this fantastic offer. Instead she went to the library and looked for books in the marriage section. There she found one that correlated men's success as husbands or fathers and their occupation. She found nothing under physicist, but she came upon one for chemical engineers. They were excellent prospects and she reasoned that "Chem-E" was close enough to physics. She then checked with her father. He had come to the U. S. in 1898, a time when Japan and China were mortal enemies. His answer was, "Marry whoever you want, but make sure he's not Chinese."

I was a penniless student, living at the sub-poverty level on $111.11 each month from the G. I. Bill. Louise dug into her savings from the twenty dollars a month stipend she received from the Cadet Nurse Corps. Lou thought we'd be rolling in dough because she would be a graduate nurse and could get a job at the hospital. As it turned out, she had to pay back one month's worth of make-up time, at twenty dollars per month, before she could qualify as a nurse. That was the time that had accrued while she was in California arranging for her mother's funeral and finding a place for her father. He had just come out of the Relocation Center to find his home burned to the ground along with all of his possessions.

But she had enough saved to buy the rings and pay all the wedding expenses. My only expenses were a suit and a pair of pajamas. When Louise asked my roommate what I was doing, he said, "He's ironing his pajamas."

The only relatives who attended our wedding were Louise's father and my younger sister, Ayako who was a nursing student in Quincy, Illinois. Louise's father refused to take off his rain boots because they were too hard to put back on. All the other guests were college classmates. We were astounded by the lavish gifts the poor students gave us: toasters, clocks, dishes, a pressure cooker and one pillow. We used that pillow for about ten years before we bought a second one. Maybe that one pillow was the cause of all those surprising pregnancies.

After the ceremony, we went to the King Cole Hotel. We could afford only one night's stay and didn't go out to eat. Instead, we dined on a box of Ritz Crackers and Limburger cheese. And then we were too worried about running up more expenses, so we moved into our new home.

This was a house we had rented with another student couple. The house had only one bathroom, and it was off the master bedroom. We were on the second floor. Nighttime trips to the bathroom were incredibly inconvenient since we had to go down a flight of stairs and through the other couple's bedroom to reach it.

To solve the toilet problem, Lou asked me to buy a pan to use as a chamber pot. I bought a small one, thinking that Louise, at eighty-nine pounds, would have a small bladder. She filled that pot in one sitting.

We had applied for admission to University Village, where veterans were housed, and were on the waiting list. This village had barracks and Quonsets for families with children and trailers for those who were childless. After about four months, a vacancy opened up, and we were able to move into a trailer.

It was a wonderful moment. We had a kerosene heater, a hot plate and two sofas that opened up into beds. The showers and bathrooms were about 200 feet away. What luxury!

UNIVERSITY VILLAGE

The men in the village became instant friends because of the shared communal latrine. The same thing happened with the women. Eventually we met the neighbors as couples. Our social life developed as we played basketball and exchanged dinners at each other's trailers.

Our closest neighbors were Bob and Lorraine Lowry. Bob was a sailor, so things were "starboard," the latrine was a "head," cleaning the house was "swabbing the deck," and junk foods were "geedunks". Bob mopped his trailer daily because a strange stench had developed. The smell never went away until Bob noticed that he was flicking his cigarette ashes into the pan on the space heater. This pan was filled with water to increase the room's humidity, but the ashes were cooking and turning the water into a stinking brew of brown juice.

And then Louise told me she was pregnant with a due date thirteen months after our wedding day. She insisted on working right through her pregnancy as a special duty nurse—a demanding assignment that paid almost twice as much as a floor nurse job. She weighed just eighty-nine pounds when we were married, and it was frightening to see her growing enormously. When she began having contractions, she timed the periods, and when she thought she was ready, she packed her bag, walked to the corner, and rode the inter-campus streetcar to the University Hospital.

Lou called me to say, "This may take some time since I'm a primipara, so wait at home and study. Somebody will call you."

That happened twelve hours later. She had given birth to Kathryn Ellen Nomura, who weighed in at six-and-a-half pounds and was nineteen inches long.

When my classmate, Bill Hanson, heard about Lou taking herself to the hospital, he chastised me. "What kind of an animal are you? When she's ready to come home, we'll get her with my car."

A couple of days later, Bill drove me to the hospital and we went to the infant viewing room. When he saw Kathi, he was most surprised. "Why, she's a Japanese baby," he said.

To this ridiculous observation, I retorted, "When you plant radishes, you get radishes and not carrots or cabbage. What the hell did you expect?"

When we brought her into our tiny quarters, she pooped. The stench was terrible and we both ran out of the trailer before coming to our senses to do what parents naturally do: change the baby's diaper! Lou instructed me to rinse out the diaper in the latrine. I did so dutifully, but created a mess by throwing up.

DO-IT-YOURSELF RULES

With the arrival of Kathi, we were able to move into one of the barracks in the University Village. We were pretty comfortable there except in the summer when the heat was ferocious. The only way we had to cool the place was to open the doors and hope for a breeze. The problem with this was that Minnesota has mosquitoes. In fact, Minnesota is famous for its giant mosquitoes. Some refer to them as the state bird. To keep those insects out while letting fresh air in, I decided to build screen doors.

I measured the height and width of the double door entry and cut my lumber and screen to size. Betty Haggstrom, our neighbor across the sidewalk from us came to check out my flurry of activity and decided that she also needed screen doors.

I assumed she'd follow my lead and measure her doorways. But no. She didn't measure anything. Instead she glued several sheets of newspaper together, cutting them into a pattern of the opening. My sense of male superiority soared to new heights as I sneered silently, "Dumb woman. She thinks she's building a dress."

But I was dismayed to find, when I had finished hanging my doors, that they didn't fit. After measuring again, with care, I discovered that the opposite sides were not equal and, further, that none of the angles were ninety degrees.

Disgruntled, I returned to the lumberyard to get more wood. (Some of the pieces had been cut too short.) While I was disassembling the doors, Betty came over to ask if I would mind stopping long enough to look at her doors to see if she had done anything wrong.

Suppressing all signs of blood pressure at 300 millimeters, I strolled over to look at her newly hung doors. The saw cuts looked as if they'd been hacked with an ax, and many of the nails were bent. On top of that, the doors were trapezoids.

But they fit with a uniform spacing of 1/16-inch all the way around. I swallowed a gallon of bile and croaked, "Betty, those are fine doors."

This story has produced two rules:

Buildings are constructed with no parallel lines or surfaces.

There are no straight lines, and none are vertical or horizontal. There are no right angles.

Measure twice and cut once.

KATHI

When I look at my children, I am amazed they aren't deformed or mentally defective because we were such ignorant parents. Unlike animals and birds that know by instinct how to care for their young, we inherited no such wisdom. We had only common sense and Dr. Spock to guide us. For example, when Kathi ran a fever of 104° F., common sense suggested that we dunk her in cold water. Her temperature dropped like a rock, but I'm sure the American Medical Association (AMA) would not recommend this procedure.

All our kids were born in Minneapolis while we were living in the University Village. At first, when we only had Kathi, Lou sterilized everything and created a sterile field for her to play in. These precautions became laughable as we had more kids, and we really did have more kids. We became like hamsters and had a stream of four children in five years. Lou was pregnant and barefooted most of the time. With the last child, she had a hysterectomy. So she probably set the record of menstruating only twice after getting married.

We no longer sterilized anything. For instance, we washed the nipples and milk bottles with the rest of the dishes. Indeed, we even put their pills on the floor since the kids put everything in their mouths. We were learning to deal with chaos.

When Kathi was only two years old, we sent her to a pre-nursery run by the University of Minnesota, College of Education. Every day she came back with a BM report pinned to her snowsuit. I learned that bowel movements come in seven colors, four consistencies and five sizes. Kathi was proud of that report and insisted that we read it carefully.

Kathi went to a speech class for her lisp under the tutelage of Elaine Argetsinger. The kid told us that Johnny Smith said, "It's time for peach class."

"How should he have said it?" I asked.

"Thilly Dad. He should have said 'thpeach' class."

She came home and recited her exercises which went, "gamma gamma guchi no so rimbo. . ."

It was hard to see how this gibberish corrected lisping, but Kathi did overcome her speech defect. Many years later, we drove north with Kathi and Elaine, who was then about eighty; both of them were sitting in the back seat of the car. They had a great time reciting "noso rimbo, gamma. . ." at the top of their lungs.

Kathi attended Oberlin College in Ohio. During the summer after her sophomore year, she worked as a counselor at a girl's camp for black kids from Harlem, New York. She wrote us an eleven-page letter describing how she knew more about the black culture than her own. She proposed that we allow her to study in Japan for her junior year.

We agreed, so she went to Tokyo to study Japanese intensively. She objected to learning the Chinese characters because she thought it was a stupid and complicated way to communicate. More importantly, she was offended by the Japanese disdain for the culturally ignorant Japanese-Americans. After becoming somewhat proficient in spoken Japanese, she undertook the study of Chinese, first in Tokyo and then in Taiwan. It is through the study of this language that she learned the Chinese characters. She returned and went to the University of Minnesota for the summer. There she met an enterprising young Japanese man who was working on his Ph.D. in Material Science. Very shortly afterward, he proposed marriage.

Kathi stood at the foot of my bed late one evening and declared, "I'm going to marry Masaki."

I pried open my eyes, pulled the pillow over my head and moaned, "Okay, go ahead."

Subsequently, our son John gave Masaki friendly advice. "You don't know what you're getting into by marrying my sister." Masaki ignored that traitor.

Kathi returned to Taiwan to complete her studies before getting married. When she was ready to come home, she sent us a letter asking us to organize a wedding for them on December 23rd, which was our twenty-fifth wedding anniversary.

"Masaki will have someone take care of the food, and Masaki and I will 'design' the ceremony," she said. She came roaring home in a cab just before the wedding.

"Pay the cabbie, will you please? I have only twenty-five cents left."

"What happened to that $1,000 cashier's check I sent you?" I asked.

"I couldn't find it," she replied. Five years later, that check turned up in her suitcase.

Kathi and Masaki lived in Japan for twelve years, had three children and studied Chinese literature. Masaki then transferred to Pittsburgh, PA to work for ALCOA. While raising her family, Kathi obtained a Ph.D. in Education from the University of Pittsburgh. Seeing the hard life of academic hopefuls up close, she decided to back out early. Instead she opted for practicing healing arts such as shiatsu, tai chi and yoga. Healing suited her better.

TERI

I was working hard during the day, and always loved coming home and finding the kids. I remember how Teri used to greet me when she was three. I used to bend down to say hello to her. She thought that bending down was part of the greeting so she would bend even lower with her greetings. Then I had to bend lower still to reach her.

Teri took after her mother and was smaller in stature than Kathi. When Teri was in the first grade, I wondered why she played with such big kids. Lou explained to me that those were her class-mates and that they were standard-size children. "Teri is small," she said. "But that doesn't matter. Children play with one another not according to size, but by age. That gives a better alignment of interests and capabilities."

When we moved to Palm Beach in the early 1960's, Ron and Marge Williams, our neighbors to the west, became our best friends. We made camping trips to various parts of Southern Florida with our families. They had two daughters who fit in the age group of our four kids, and it made for a nice vacation for all of us.

Once, when our two cars were heading down the road toward the Everglades National Park, Lou suddenly remembered that she'd forgotten to pick up sugar for our coffee.

"We can't go back now," I said. "We passed the last grocery store two hours ago."

"That's all right," she replied. "We'll just stop for coffee at the next restaurant and pick up a few packages of sugar from the container."

Sounded good to me, so we all trooped into the restaurant and sat down. When the waitress brought the menu, their five-year-old piped up.

"We didn't come for breakfast. We came to get some of your bags of sugar."

Suddenly there were four adults with beet-red faces. Without discussion, we placed our orders for our unintended breakfast.

Later, Ron and I agreed that if we were going to steal anything, we'd make it worthwhile by stealing at least a million dollars. Especially if we didn't think the person would miss it.

When Teri was in the seventh grade, she asked me how to take the square root of a number. I outlined the algorithm on the blackboard and gave a geometric interpretation. I proceeded with more of the same for the cube root, and wrapped up with nifty methods for extracting any root of any number.

After stifling fifty yawns, she said, "I really didn't want to know that much."

Since then she has never asked me how to do anything. Teri grew up without my help.

When I was reassigned back to Minneapolis, we left the kids behind in Florida with the lady next door while we went house hunting in Minneapolis. Teri was six months delinquent in a science project, so she persuaded our lady baby sitter to allow her to stay home so that she could do her project. When we got home about a week later, Teri was a celebrity. She had not only taken first prize for her cytology exhibit at school, but she took first for the entire Palm Beach County. When the press interviewed her, they asked if she intended to become a biologist.

"No," she said, "I hate biology."

Teri told me when she was about an eighth grader that she wanted to become a chemist when she grew up. I got her a chemistry set. Then, just before Christmas, I decided I should give her a better one than that. So I gave the first one to John, who was very pleased with the gift, but I also made the catastrophic mistake of forgetting to buy Teri her bigger and better set.

This was naturally a great disappointment to Teri, but she didn't mention it until fifteen years later.

Mea culpa, mea culpa, mea maxima culpa. I will carry that mistake with me to my grave.

Parents, pay heed to your children and follow through with your promises. They are telling you important things!

High school years were happy times for Teri at University High. She was famous for her parties. The number of guests was never clear because her invitation was: "We're having a party at my place, pass the word." One hundred fifty kids would show up complete with at least two bands. When the drummers beat the drums, the amplifiers drew so much current that the neighborhood lights dimmed. When the neighbors complained, they were invited, so Teri got away with murder. She graduated with honors and then went on to the University of Minnesota.

One day Teri brought home her boy friend and explained to me how they were going to live. My response was "Holy Mackerel, gasp, choke, you mean cohabit?"

In time I recovered from my fourteen heart attacks, rounded off a few sharp, square corners and life went on.

My greatest disappointment in Teri is that she does not allow me the privilege, as a father, to be proud of her. For example, she graduated with a Bachelor of Fine Arts (BFA) in art, *Summa Cum Laude* and a *Phi Beta Kappa* but she didn't go to her graduation on the grounds that "all that Mickey Mouse wasn't worth twenty-five bucks." I could not bask in the glory of her achievements that only a miniscule percentage of people could ever attain. To compensate for all the fuss I created, she went through the whole nine yards for my benefit when she got her Master of Arts (MA).

As a final act of defiance to the system, she gave her academic robe to the Art Department with instructions to let succeeding generations of MA graduates use the gown to save the "Twenty-seven dollar rip-off for the Mickey Mouse ceremony."

Teri turned out to be a chip off the old block. I found this out when we attended a self-awareness workshop. In one of the assignments, we had to draw something on the blackboard depicting creativity. We were twenty feet apart from each other so we couldn't see what the other was doing, but we drew the identical diagram.

Teri wanted to marry a hippie. So, on June 28, 1983, two days after her birthday, she married Mike Bowen, a bona fide hippie. At first Mike wanted to move to Grand Marais, Minnesota, away from the noise and crowds and be very close to the soil. I think Teri dragged her feet until the "Washington" idea came up. They had friends in Washington, so they went for a two-year trial. That trial ended when they started building their house in Port Hadlock. Then Sumiko was born on June 18, 1986. What a lucky girl to have Teri and Mike for parents!

I am very fortunate to have Teri for a daughter. I burst with pride because she does good things for people. She does things creatively and with high energy and purpose and she is not stymied by seemingly impossible tasks. She excels in art and her values are correct for they include conservation and ecology. She is great.

JOHN

John was a mother's delight, for he never drooled or got dirty. He did his mischief quietly. When he was about five, he climbed up on the washing machine, opened the fuse box without a protection shield and unscrewed every fuse. When I got home, I noticed that the kids in the neighborhood were playing with fuses. It was easy to figure out where they came from because none of the lights worked. He missed execution by electricity by only a quarter of an inch. On another occasion, he became interested in my electric drill and knocked holes everywhere including every one of the chairs of our brand new dining set.

When we lived in Florida, he found a Cottonmouth snake. Our friends, thinking we were snake lovers began giving us snakes. Pretty soon we had an aquarium full. Then one got away and disappeared somewhere in the house. Since I wouldn't touch those slimy looking things with a fifty-one-foot pole, I hated going into the house without checking the bed and the sofa ten times over. After two months of precarious living, we found the rascal sleeping under a pile of newspapers. I instructed John to get rid of all of them, thus killing his interest in those reptiles.

When he was a teenager, he and Dave (our youngest son), found a dynamite cap. They put it in the alley, next to a cement retaining wall behind our house. They lined up several rocks on top of the wall then pushed off each rock one by one, hoping to hit the dynamite cap. They had about fifty misses but finally one landed squarely on the cap. It went off with a resounding crack and filled half a block of the alley with dust. In the meantime, I came home just in time to greet two policemen at our door who were investigating the explosion. I said I didn't know about any explosion so they went away. John stood behind me saying nothing and looking innocent. The scene was reminiscent of the time I shot a man with a slingshot. The difference was that I was caught but John, the rat, got away with it. He didn't tell me this story until he was fifty years old!

When he finished junior high, he announced, "I have decided to go to college. What do I have to know?"

"You need three skills," I replied, "reading comprehension, writing and speaking."

The simplicity of my answer puzzled him, "How about subjects like math?"

"That is learned mostly by having skills in reading comprehension," I answered. "Math is no different than cooking. If you understand what you read you should be able to handle any level of math or make any exotic cuisine."

I don't know if I convinced him, but he signed up for a speech class at the University of Minnesota during the summer vacation and loved it. When he returned to high school in the fall, he got straight A's, perhaps because he was motivated by his decision to go to college. He graduated with honors and chose Grinnell College. He majored in American Studies and then psychology and was on the dean's list for scholastic achievements.

But disenchantment crept in. He computed the cost of his education by the month, week, day and finally by the hour and decided that it wasn't worth it because he didn't know where he was headed. He quit and came home.

Then one day he said, "I'm going to Berkeley to study psychology. Will you give me your VW bug and some tools?"

He took an odd selection of socket wrenches out of my toolbox. I don't think they fit very well, because all of my tools were American Standard, while every nut on the VW was metric. He wanted no financial support since he intended to make it on his own. He disappeared into California.

He then learned about Chinese medicine, acupuncture and holistic medicine. From that he shifted to respiratory therapy, a treatment for those with lung related ailments.

At that point, I went to California to find out what he was doing. I proposed, "If you are interested in making people well, why don't you become a medical doctor?" He wanted no part of the medical profession.

A young lady convinced him that real estate was the way to go. He came home and began working as a real estate agent while supporting himself as a respiratory therapist. He said he could enjoy the satisfaction of matching a client with the ideal. But he sold nothing for many months and, when he finally did complete a sale, he decided that he disliked both respiratory therapy and real estate.

I suggested that he take the *Strong-Campbell Vocational Interest Test.* I had taken the same test twice, forty years apart, with the same results, namely that I would probably succeed in math, physics, medicine or public administration, and that my highest interest was adventure.

John took the test and found out that he was more interested in things than people and that his profile of interests matched most closely to computer programmers.

This outcome pleased him so he went back to the University of Minnesota and began taking algebra, then calculus I through calculus VI. Simultaneously, he took the computer science sequence. In the meantime, he obtained an internship at Honeywell that paid for his education. This took about three years, but he graduated *Summa Cum Laude* and was elected to *Phi Beta Kappa.* Like Teri, before him, he too denied me the privilege of being proud of him by not going to his graduation.

When I showed him the draft of what I wrote about him, he crossed out everything I said about his impressive achievements. That didn't deter me. I chose to say whatever I pleased because this was going to be *my* book. I denied him all editorial rights!

Through this long odyssey of dabbling in lots of fields, he became very broadly educated.

John went to work for Honeywell as a Software Engineer for a screwy reason: "I liked the people I worked with."

"That's a dumb reason," I argued. "Go to work for a company whose mainstream business is software, such as Microsoft."

But he was adamant and delved into developing software for Honeywell. John was probably hired for life just like his father.

John has always had a penchant for Chinese women. The father of one of the girls he dated in Berkeley liked him and paid the highest praise he knew: "Why, you look more Chinese than Japanese."

This inclination proved to be his greatest blessing, for he married Wen Sheng. He met her at a dinner set up by his work-mate. She was a graduate student from Taiwan, working on her Ph.D. in plant physiology and biochemistry at Virginia Polytechnic Institute in Virginia. Her nickname is Sunny, which truly reflects her disposition.

John and Sunny were married in Minneapolis on September 30, 1989. At that time, Sunny had finished her research. She then brought home all her data, sat down and wrote her dissertation, defended it, and received her doctorate. A cockatiel also accompanied this marriage. What a coup! Sunny is brilliant, kind, considerate and pretty besides. She is a most loved member of the family.

After the wedding, she wanted to call me Dr. Nomura as custom required from her Chinese upbringing. I said, "No, call me Carl." She thought it over for one night and came back with the proposal, "I can't call you Carl and Louise. Let me call you mom and dad."

As mentioned elsewhere in this book, John also became the peacemaker and our advisor on marriage and getting along. I have profited from lots of good advice from him. Lately, he's been giving me advice on staying healthy. My reaction is, "If I have to eat the unappetizing stuff you live on, it's a life not worth living. I like food too much." Indeed, I live to eat and not the other way around. But I confess, he is very healthy and he doesn't have an ounce of fat on him.

He came to see me recently and looked at my homemade bench press and advised, "The depression is over. Get yourself some decent equipment." Now I have a fancy Schwinn exercising system. In no time, I'll cease being a ninety-seven-pound weakling and have bulging muscles.

DAVID

The obstetrician kept saying, "I feel two heads." But Lou didn't have the presence of mind to ask if he also felt two bodies. "Were we going to have a baby with two heads," I groaned." Lou finally asked and learned that it was a benign tumor, the type that would shrink away during the menopausal years.

The doctor decided to do a cesarean section surgery because the tumor obstructed the birth canal. He invited me to watch the procedure from the medical students' gallery above the operating table. The surgeon began stabbing her with his injection instrument that looked much like an oil gun excepting that it had a syringe sticking out of the side. He probably had about a pint of Novocain and he jabbed, pulled the trigger, jabbed and pulled the trigger, thirty to forty times to cover the entire abdominal area. When the numbing drug took effect, the doctor started cutting from the navel down. As he cut the exterior layer, he pulled it back with forceps and clamped it. Then he started to cut the next layer. I remember nothing else because I fainted. When I came to, a nurse said, "It's a boy."

Lou, on the other hand, asked the operating nurse to adjust the mirror so she could watch the operation. I guess she was able to watch because she was a nurse who saw blood and guts every day. He removed the tumor, removed the baby and did a partial hysterectomy.

Later, the doctor saw Louise weighing herself and then devouring a chicken dinner. He exploded with, "This is a sacrilege! Don't you know you died on the table and that I had to resuscitate you back to life?" She answered nonchalantly, "Yes, I know. I saw myself dead from the corner ceiling of the operating room. I had an out of body experience." In later years, she used to kid David about being born after he was.

Had David been born two months earlier, I would have taken a job at Bell Laboratories in Murray Hill, NJ. Instead, I stayed in Minneapolis. How different our lives would have been. We would have had different friends. Each of our children would have married someone else, and they would have had different children.

David was the youngest child and therefore was at the bottom of the pecking order. Susie, our dachshund was the only member of the family that Dave outranked. His older brother and sisters were too big to confront but he found a way of getting even. When the older three children watched television, they gave it undivided attention. Dave kicked each kid knowing that no one would bother to hit him back.

Dave had a hamster named Snoopy that he dearly loved. It got out of his cage and like all rodents, Snoopy ran along the wall. Not seeing him, I stepped on him when I came down from a ladder. I was so sorry seeing that flattened pet, I offered to buy another one. That wasn't good enough. He wanted me to restore Snoopy. Forty years have elapsed and I wonder if Dave has forgiven me. I must ask him.

When he was little, Dave was very quiet most of the time and showed little evidence of mischief. When we packed all the furniture to move to Florida, we found a few dozen treasures that he drew and hid behind furniture, on doorjambs and in other inaccessible places that only a six-year-old could creep into.

Dave always carried around a monkey doll made from a stocking. Once when driving from Minnesota to Florida, Dave threw a few tantrums. On one of these, he was so angry that he threw his beloved monkey out of the window, expecting me to stop to retrieve it. To teach him the folly of tantrums, I drove on and on as he grieved more and more. That doll was gone forever. After he had children, this became a legendary family story. For his forty-fifth birthday, his wife, Veda, made him a replica of that monkey. That treasure rests atop his bedstead. Every time I saw it, I felt I must buy a plastic ducky wucky for my bathtub. (I no longer yearn for it, I have one floating in my tub.)

To our great pleasure Dave turned out to be an outstanding student with no inducement or encouragement from us. If the school was giving any kind of award, he was one of the winners. He went to Carleton College in Northfield, Minnesota and majored in math. He was used to being at the head of the class, but at Carleton he learned that most of his classmates were scholarly valedictorians. He received his first "C."

He became concerned about the cost of his education so he went to summer schools at the University of Minnesota. He then took eighteen to twenty credits at Carleton and managed to graduate in two and one half years. Nevertheless, he still graduated *Magna cum laude* and was elected to *Phi Beta Kappa*. He went through the whole graduation ceremony for my benefit, unlike his siblings.

After graduation he went to the University of Wisconsin and majored in computer science. After six years of graduate work, he called to say, "I'm tired of school. What's a good company to work for in Portland, Oregon?" I said, "Intel." He kissed off his shot at a Ph.D. and moved to Portland. In my days, we found a job first and went wherever the company was located.

One summer he worked at Camp Unistar as a co-cook with Veda Melvin. This immediately became a tutor/apprentice relationship since Veda was an excellent cook while Dave's only expertise was warming up pizzas. He boldly claimed that if you can read, you should be able to make anything. Once when following a recipe that called for a cup of baking powder he mistakenly used baking soda and made the cuisine inedible. Nevertheless, he and Veda put on artistic and theatrical dinners. Once for an Italian dinner, they had a guest who happened to be an opera singer. This guest sang while the staff served the meal, wearing fancy paper cuffs. (Normally they served the campers from the counter.)

David's finest achievement was marrying Veda for she is a scholar, an organizer, homemaker and a great mother. For evidence of David's "finest achievement," I just point to the outstanding children she and David reared.

Since Dave was the family athlete, winning letters in four sports, it's not surprising to discover that he now runs to and from work to keep in shape. When he reached middle age, he discovered golf. Veda warned me, "You don't joke about golf with David."

It is hard for a proud parent to be modest about him.

MARRIAGE COUNSELING

I grew up as a member of a dysfunctional family. My father caused many traumas with his spoiled, childish behavior. He deposited the four older children at the doorsteps of disinterested relatives, didn't send money as he promised, then brought them home and beat them, as he beat the rest of us. His death was a relief to us all.

Louise, on the other hand, lived the life of a pampered princess. She and her siblings were loved. Her father was the kindest and most generous person I ever met. When her hometown decided to have a town reunion, former residents came from afar. Many people sought out Louise to thank her for the wonderful and kind things her father had done for them during the depression years.

Once, when Lou was about three months pregnant, she walked toward a chair to sit down. Her father grabbed a cushion and in an instant placed it under his daughter before her bottom could hit the chair. Such an extreme act of thoughtfulness would never have occurred to me.

Clearly, strange things were destined to happen when we married. We took the *Myers-Briggs* test and found we were exact opposites. I tested as an introverted- intuitive-thinking-judgmental-person (INTJ), while Lou was an extroverted-sensing-feeling-perceiving-person (ESFP). We were cast in concrete that way. This was supposed to be perfect for marriages, according to Myers and Briggs. Methinks there is a flaw in their reasoning, because "opposite" should mean that we would disagree on everything. But not only were we opposites, Lou was also a random thinker while I am linear. Thus, she was apt to go from A to P to E to Z while I would insist on moving logically from A to B to C to D. The chances of good communication between us was always remote. With our backgrounds and different makeups, could our marriage succeed?

I thought we were doing pretty well. But, after twenty years, Louise decided that our marriage was defective and needed corrections. She noticed in the *Minneapolis Star Journal* that the city provided marriage counseling at the courthouse free of charge.

On the appointed day, she went to the place where a psychologist listened to people who related their problems and received solutions. Lou was sitting fourth in line, looking for wise advice from the oracle. She couldn't help hearing those ahead of her as they revealed their problems. The first case involved a young woman of twenty, pregnant and holding a baby while trying to console a child of about three who was screeching for attention.

"My husband was in a motorcycle accident," she began. "He had to have both knee caps removed, and now he can't walk. And because he's unskilled, he can't get a job. I'm unable to work because I'm about to have a baby, and I have to nurse my little girl. What can I do?"

The counselor explained the welfare system and then gave her the phone number of the social worker she should contact.

In the second case, a woman about forty years old held a baby while wiping the nose of a second child, a girl of about two. She explained, "My eighteen-year-old daughter ran away leaving me her two children. The baby is mentally retarded and requires my full attention. My husband is the father of this child but he won't give support money either to our daughter or to me. I have to go to work to take care of these kids, but I can't afford a baby-sitter. What can I do?"

The solution for this woman was the same as for the previous case.

The next woman looked down at the floor to hide her blackened eyes. She hobbled up to the chair in front of the psychologist's desk, straightened her ragged clothes and began: "My husband comes home once in a while and beats me. I've got to keep him away before he starts hurting the kids while he's drunk. I get welfare help for my children and myself, but my husband comes home to steal the money from me. The police won't help . . ."

Before this woman had finished explaining her problem, Louise left.

She told me later, "I would have felt foolish saying my problem is that my husband doesn't call me from work to say hello."

But she wasn't giving up. We then went to a man with such a new Master of Social Work (MSW) degree that his shingle was still dripping wet paint. We were his *first* customers. He listened to our grievances for about five minutes apiece and then pointed his finger at Louise. "You're the problem," he said.

What an incredible performance! In just ten minutes he thought he had solved difficulties we hadn't been able to unravel after trying for decades.

In retrospect, of course, he erred. It wasn't that Lou was wrong. It was that I spent a lot of time developing and rehearsing what I was going to say, while Lou gave the matter little thought and shot from the hip. He judged incorrectly because he didn't take into account the difference in our levels of preparation. I fooled him with convincing logic and eloquence.

After this disastrous experience, we sought counseling from a famous psychiatrist who had his own practice at a medical center attached to a mental institution. With a vision of a zombie-eyed Jack Nicholson in *One Flew Over the Cuckoo's Nest,* we walked cautiously into the doctor's office and sat down staring at him. Looking like a high society doctor with crisp and careful language, he described his procedure.

"Carl will speak about his grievances and I'll explain to Louise what he meant. Then we'll reverse roles. I'll be your translator. Neither of you may respond unless I say it is okay."

This went on for several sessions. Nothing calamitous happened, and it was not clear to us where we were headed. At the fifth session, he said, "Now I'm going to speak to you separately."

Louise went first and reported that he took a lot of notes but gave no counsel. When my turn came, I asked, "When are you going to teach us how to speak to one another without having you as a go-between?"

With a surprised look he said, "I don't know how to do that."

We quit because the prospect of having him as an interpreter for the rest of our lives didn't solve our problem of poor communication. The lesson we learned from this doctor was the importance of listening to the other's grievances all the way through without interrupting, becoming catatonic, or threatening mayhem.

We then went to an encounter group, a form of therapy that was very popular in the seventies. Since there were about thirty of us, we divided into three circles and made sure that spouses were in different groups. We took turns introducing ourselves and saying something about our marriages. One man in my circle announced that, in thirty years of marriage, he and his wife had never had an argument. To prove his claim, he yelled two circles away: "Hey, Madge, we never had an argument, right?"

She answered dutifully, "Yes, dear."

Louise, sitting in the circle next to mine, described my defects eloquently. "As an example, when I prepare a beautiful roast beef dinner, he'll bring out a jar of peanut butter as though what I prepared wasn't good enough."

I shrank and looked into the distance, hoping nobody in my

circle heard her recitation of how rotten I was.

When she finished, a white-haired woman expressed her opinion in a piercing voice. "If he likes peanut butter, he can't be all that bad."

Everyone in the room heard her and guffawed.

During the break, I ran over to the lady, thanked her and gave her a hug for saving me.

After three days, we left with some good ideas on how to have a better marriage, but I don't now remember what they were. The obnoxious man who never argued with his wife left after the first day, since the conference had nothing to teach him. His slave-wife followed her lord back to their perfect marriage.

The best counseling came from our son with support from his siblings. John, our third child, assumed the role of the peacemaker in the family. He couldn't stand the constant yelling and screaming, so he sat Louise and me at opposite ends of our dining table. The four teenagers sat between us and took charge. John explained the rules:

"Mom and Dad are going to speak, one at a time. The other cannot interrupt unless I say it's all right. Say whatever it is that's bugging you. Continue speaking until you have nothing left to say."

It was wonderful. We brought out all the old tapes and screamed our grievances without argument or correction. I rejoiced, for I had never had such a freewheeling session in all my life.

We then had a chance to answer without the other saying, "But . . .but . . ."

Lou got her chance to crucify me. After having a field day yelling about what was wrong, we began wondering what we were complaining about. Now every grievance seemed pitifully small.

Maybe we just had to clear our sinuses.

John concluded that we had a big house with too much to do. He explained, "The burden of getting things done falls on Mom." This was unfair. He solved the problem by making a list of all the tasks that needed to be done such as buying groceries, cooking, cleaning after meals, cleaning the house, cleaning the yard, washing clothes, doing miscellaneous errands. He made a master chart for the whole month and assigned tasks to everyone. If there was a conflict, he arranged changes.

All the yelling stopped, and the house remained in tip-top condition. The best part was that, during our free time, we could goof off without feeling guilty even when someone was working hard cleaning right next to us.

For example, the designated worker who cooked the dinner expected no help from us because it was our free time. That worker knew that roles would reverse soon. The bad news was that John was going to college in a year or so, and he would be leaving behind a dysfunctional family.

We went to a conference on marriage, conducted by Dr. Gerhard Neubeck, Professor of Family Studies Center at the University of Minnesota. He summarized the situation like this:

"Marriage, even at its best, is a difficult relationship. The root cause is excessive expectations. When young men look at young women, they perceive healthy, bright, well-educated, thoughtful and capable people. The women's perceptions of men are the same. When they marry, they unconsciously begin leaning on one another. To their amazement, they begin passing each other with little support."

What a surprising conclusion from an expert who had studied thousands of marriages for over thirty years! No wonder marriages require so much help.

One interpretation of Dr. Neubeck's advice is that we should try to meet the other's needs completely. I gave it a shot. I did everything Louise wanted done. If she wanted shelves, I galvanized into action and finished the job quickly. I even went one step better by doing the job twice as fine as she expected. One monument sat in our front yard; it was a small arched bridge that I built without nails. It took two days, and its workmanship far surpassed her expectations.

Did the idea of doing whatever Lou wanted work? From her vantage point, the answer was "Yes," for she basked in seventh heaven when I met her every need. This illustrates what I call my principle of the *Conservation of Happiness*. My unhappiness offsets her happiness exactly, so that the total happiness in the universe remained unchanged.

I thought I understood what was going on, but I was wrong. I happened to hear Louise tell a friend, "I accidentally ran our car over that miniature bridge Carl made for me. Oh well, the arch was too high, anyway."

It was an accident, so that was all right. But I had been wrong about the bridge being twice as good as she expected. It didn't even meet her specs—it was too high! The lesson I learned from this was: if a spouse wants something demanding done, hire someone to do it.

As we feared, when John left for college, we became dysfunctional again. At first it didn't appear so, for there were only three of us left, and later only two when the youngest left for college. The enemy was my job. I was a workaholic, and I traveled a lot. The few days I was home, I could shove problems under the rug and then go off to work again.

The traveling, however, may have saved our marriage, because we looked pretty good during the short times we were together.

The travel separations disappeared when I retired. Suddenly I was home all the time, which gave us the opportunity to fight constantly. We weren't fighting about any of the traditional problems outlined in *The Reader's Digest* or *Ladies' Home Journal,* such as money, child rearing, religion, politics or sex. Money held no interest for Louise. Once, when I summarized our current and projected incomes and assets in case I died, she listened for a while, yawned, and asked me if there was more. I droned on for a couple of minutes, then she asked me if there was more again. I started up again and she stopped me. "Just tell me if I'm going to be okay or not."

I said, "You'll be okay."

Lou went back to her sculpture.

With the kids, we did it Lou's way. Her theories were brilliant. She told the kids, "This is your life to live as you please. Go to college or don't go. Choose your lifestyle and your occupation."

She also believed that kids learn only from mistakes. I protested. "Why not stand on the shoulders of experience and avoid doing dumb things?"

I winced, but went along with her. The children could never play one of us against the other because we were a united front. No matter which parent they asked, they got the same answer. She called her style "benign neglect" because, although she looked like she wasn't paying attention, she was in reality watching every child very closely.

I think Lou's theories were correct because our children all emerged honor students, they are doing work they like, they are good parents, and they have good kids.

On religion and politics, our differences were too negligible to argue about. As for sex, it was fantastic almost all the time.

For years, I offered the simple solution of doing things the way they were done in Japan: it was her cultural heritage to take care of and be subservient to her husband. As a Japanese woman, she should have been referring to me as "My master." Unfortunately for me, Lou didn't buy into any of those great traditions that had been developed over thousands of years.

The reason for this became clear when I met Lou's family. They were Samurai, the fiercest warriors Japan ever produced. No wonder she was so strong! She had warrior genes. While I, with genes inherited from peaceful poets, seek only harmony.

GETTING ALONG IN MARRIAGE

At a luncheon, a woman sitting next to me whispered, "Tomorrow is our wedding anniversary, but I'm not going to tell my husband. I think he's forgotten it. He hasn't given a clue. If he forgets tomorrow, I'm going to kill him."

I looked at the victim, seated across and two seats to the left. He was wolfing down Chinese food. The poor guy didn't know that the sword of Damocles hung over his head by the finest spider thread, ready to cleave him in two. He looked too busy to be thinking about an event that had taken place forty-one years before. June 27th is a day of no significance with anything attached to trigger his memory. So the poor man barely survived from year to year because he played Russian roulette with his wedding anniversary.

I had the immense good fortune to have married on December 23, 1947, the day on which Bardeen and Brattain invented the transistor. I, therefore, never failed to remember our anniversary, for all I had to do was think "transistor" or "John Bardeen" and "anniversary" would pop into my head.

This device saved me from peril forty-nine times in a row. Yet despite the fidelity with which I remembered the momentous day, I was no better off than the man who never remembered. My excellent track record did not impress Louise because my memory aid was as cold and inert as $E = mc^2$. She yearned for a basis such as the first kiss, moonlight and roses and other romantic clichés. Unfortunately, I couldn't change because transistors and Bardeen are so firmly imbedded in my consciousness.

A GREAT MARRIAGE, FINALLY

Lou and I always had tried to solve all our problems at once and we kept failing at it. So I began asking, "What problems could possibly remain?" We decided the resolution of the apparently trivial arguments that kept leading to cataclysms was to overcome them one fault at a time. After forty-eight years of marriage, I concluded that we had two faults:

First, we were discourteous to each other. For example, she contradicted me with points of no consequence, as in:

"It was Wednesday, not Tuesday."

"No, it was Tuesday."

"Wednesday."

"Tuesday."

We made listeners uncomfortable with those senseless arguments.

Secondly, I committed the crime of belittling Lou.

So we tried working on these two faults and only these two faults, and then, once a week, we would check in to get feedback on how well we were doing. We figured that, when we'd eliminated those two problems altogether, we'd go on to the next one.

We never did get to the third or fourth defect, though we continued working on those first two for a long time. We would fall and stumble, but the incidence of transgressions did decline. The idea definitely held promise. Why did it take forty-eight years to think of it?

Many years ago I was most impressed with Bertrand Russell's formulation of the good life: "The good life is one inspired by love and guided by knowledge."

Though brilliant, I now think love is too amorphous an idea. For example, carnal love could lead to exploitation. Agape love could become excessive preoccupation with God and not enough with your fellow man. Altruistic love is the proper starting point, but I was not sure how to initiate Russell's advice.

One day it occurred to me that the root cause of Lou and my discourtesies was that we were not kind to one another. I therefore persuaded Lou that before we got out of bed in the morning, we were to think about one kind thing we could do for each other, and then, later on, do it. For example, when I knew that she was going to have a strenuous day at the art studio, I did some of her usual chores such as cooking the dinner or cleaning the house. She noticed that I fussed a lot about losing my passport, so she made me a cloth bag that I could hang around my neck.

We never announced, "Hey, I'm going to do something kind for you." Instead, we did it quietly. But I always knew when Lou was doing a kind act for me.

We reminded ourselves often about the pledge of kindness. Though each act was small, the accumulated effects over a period of time, say one year, did make huge differences. I believe that, though my acts of kindness affected Louise, I am the one who received the greatest benefit, because I began to change a little bit each time I thought about doing something kind.

Unless I find a better one, my solution, after trying for five decades, is to *be kind to your spouse.* Though this may appear to be a trivial bit of advice, and even axiomatic, this is the best I can give. I cannot think of a possible bad consequence of being kinder, while there are possible bad consequences for loving too much. In my opinion, "Be kind to your neighbor" is a more effective teaching than "love thy neighbor." You might get shot for loving your neighbor.

I made a living for almost thirty-five years as a problem solver. I solved problems in theoretical physics and in math. I solved all kinds of management problems such as people problems, problems created by people, money problems, and production problems. Though I was successful in these areas, I was a failure at solving problems in marriage. What a tough nut to crack!

The summer of 1996, at Seabeck, a Unitarian family camp, I listened to a songwriter who composed a country western with the major theme, "From love comes kindness." I spoke to him later and said I had come to the opposite conclusion: "From kindness comes love." He was amazed, for he had never thought of this possibility. It runs contrary to traditional belief.

By a stroke of great luck, I learned that, on his deathbed, Aldous Huxley had summarized his conclusions about life with the simple statement, "Be kinder." How lucky I was to reach the same conclusion as that great man.

MY RULES FOR GETTING ALONG

1. Be kind, considerate and friendly.
2. If something is wrong, resolve it.
3. Don't ask others to do what you can do except:
   When you're too tired.

      When you're late.

      When you are too busy.

4. Speak civilly.
5. Do more than your share.
6. Don't insist you are always right we all err!

      Compromise.

      Laugh at your own mistakes.

7. Have fun!

CHAPTER VII

Minneapolis Friends

THE NEW NEIGHBORHOOD

Hopkins, Minnesota

We bought our first house in 1954. It was in Hopkins, Minnesota, a suburb of Minneapolis. Louise chose that particular house because it had robin's egg blue bathroom fixtures. Several months later, we found out that the builders had polled to see if anyone objected to having a Japanese family move in. None objected.

We soon became friendly with our neighbor, Dale Ponder, who lived next door. He was a highly skilled and a most meticulous mechanical engineer. When he mowed his lawn, he went north to south on the first cut. On the next, he went east to west. On the third run, he went diagonally and finally diagonally in the other direction. Not only that, but this perfectionist kept careful records of his lawn cutting history. His objective was to encourage every blade of grass to grow vertically rather than in some uncontrolled direction.

Dale went berserk when he made some careful measurements of an area at his house. In fact, he discovered the realities of *Do-It-*

Yourself Rule Number One. His plan was to winterize and convert his porch into a sunroom. He wanted his new space to be a perfect rectangular parallelepiped. How could he have one, if his floor diagonals were off by two inches and his ceiling wasn't level? He could not live with gross imperfections, so he set out to build a perfect room inside of his misshapen porch.

In his agitated state of mind, he discovered *Rule Number Two* when he cut his high-priced two by four studs an inch and a half too short. He could have faked it by nailing a two by four on top of his floor plates, but his psychological makeup forbade that. He bought more wood to do it right.

Three months later he moved to California leaving behind his sunroom built with a tolerance of 1/128 inch and ten seconds of arc at the corners.

The neighbor on our backside was an ace salesman. Whenever his company had any kind of sales contest, he won it. Because he was so good at selling, he had the additional duty of training the newly hired salesmen. Chuck was a taskmaster, but his pupils loved the man.

He also ruled his family with a lot of yelling, but the whole family knew there was no bite in his outraged barking. He looked and acted like Jack Nicholson, excepting that his smile was sincere. One of his pastimes was to come to my house to give me a hard time, just like he did to his trainees.

He lived in a tract house like ours, except it was a left-handed version. When I installed shutters in our front window to keep out the afternoon sun, Chuck admired the elegance of my acquisition. He had to have the same thing.

He came to my house with new shutters, measured my window and cut his shutters to size. He took them home and found to his horror that his window was two inches taller than mine. How could this happen in a tract home? Here is a man who leaped over

Rule Number One and Number Two and invented Rule Number Three: Measure the right thing before cutting.

The *Do-It-Yourself* craze emerged because people wanted to save money for the good things in life. Let me illustrate how it worked for me with a window. We had a crack in the middle of a large window of our living room. Since this house was spacious and ancient, we had become used to the eyesore.

But one Sunday, when I had nothing else to do, I decided to fix that window. The local hardware man wanted twenty dollars for the job, ten for the glass and ten for labor. I thought I could save ten dollars for this simple task.

I measured the opening and committed the dimensions to memory. On the way home from work about a week later, I had glass cut to my specifications. I marveled at how clever I was to remember the size of the window opening.

But alas, when I lifted the glass in place, it was half an inch too narrow. Undaunted, I bought a second pane, which fit perfectly. With my mouth full of those triangular things for tacking the glass in place, I stood at the top of the ladder while holding the pane. I discovered to my dismay that I left the hammer on the ground. I balanced that pane in place as I crept carefully down the ladder.

I managed to pick up the hammer and was halfway back up the ladder when my daughter, Teri, burst through the front door. "I'm home," she shouted cheerfully.

The sudden increase in pressure caused the large pane of glass to pop out and crash down on my head. It broke into a million pieces. As I brushed off the glass slivers, I murmured to my daughter, "You ought not slam open the front door when you come in."

On the third try I made it. Assuming my labor was worth nothing, I lost twenty dollars and a precious Sunday's day of rest.

MOX

Mox was a doberman pincer and, like a Grizzly Bear, he had no natural enemies. He was an arsenal of teeth and taut muscles, so that strangers and animals gave him much berth. Even watching him eat caused the timid to shrink away. He ate as though he were starved or hated having food in his mouth. He gulped down a whole can of dog food without biting once. Clearly, his joy of eating was in digesting his food rather than in savoring it.

Though he looked like a killer, he was a gentle and loving pet. He was not a show dog since he had floppy ears and a long rat-like tail. The children in the neighborhood knew his real character, so he was made a frequent participant in their parades. He always seemed to know which role he was playing. When dressed as a clown, he was full of mischief. With a crown on his head and a regal blanket draped over his back, he showed all the pomp of his Britannic Majesty.

Mox was Jim Bottomley's inseparable pet. His favorite position was with his jowls resting on Jim's knee. When not adoring his master, he liked to romp with the neighbor's miniature Collie. Being a much older dog, she didn't like rough-housing, so she'd snap at Mox. Though not meaning to, she bit Mox's ear and sliced it lengthwise into two—four inch long strips. Jim sandwiched the two parts between pieces of cardboard cut in the shape of the ear. Then he taped them together.

This heavy bandage on his ear bothered Mox, so he kept trying to scrape it off. When he was caught in the act, he'd stop instantly and assume the "Who, me? I'm not doing anything," expression. In time the ear healed perfectly, but Mox's games with the Collie became genteel.

In spite of his size, he liked climbing on people's laps—especially those of women. His technique was to test by putting a paw on his next victim's lap. If this was tolerated, he eased his whole leg onto the lap. With each smile of approval, he'd continue by putting his other front leg onto the lap, then sneak up both of his hind legs with toenails relaxed lest he scratched his warm cushion. He transferred his ninety-pound weight from the floor to the lap in graceful and barely discernible motions so that the lady became used to the ever-increasing load. Once on the lap, he rested his jowls on his front paws, smiled broadly and feigned sleep. Though spurned a hundred times, he did occasionally succeed, and he always kept trying.

Often in the summer Jim filled a knapsack with picnic food for both of them and they would take off for his swimming hole. Unfortunately, they had to scale down a wall to get to the hole, or crawl through a culvert about three feet in diameter. Mox wouldn't jump down from the wall. He also refused to walk through the culvert because he didn't like the cobwebs. Jim tried shoving him into the culvert, but Mox held his ground. Coaxing him from the other end didn't influence the stubborn animal. So Mox remained at the top of the wall and complained bitterly by yowling. Though Mox wouldn't join the fun, he always insisted on following his master.

Jim heard a local rumor that two girls went skinny-dipping in his swimming hole. The rumor seemed to be true, because he saw the lovely sixth graders going in that direction with their towels and no swimming suits. He could see the outline of their nubile breasts. With much excitement, he followed quietly and watched as the girls began to undress. At the perfectly inopportune moment, Mox chose to walk through the culvert to join the girls.

"Whose dog is that?" one of the girls asked.

"That's Jim Bottomley's dog."

Both dressed hurriedly, climbed the wall and ran back to town.

Jim's family was moving to town and planning to live in an apartment. The landlord didn't like animals, so Jim came to the difficult conclusion that they'd have to find a home for Mox. Everyone loved this dog, but nobody seemed to want him. As a last resort, Jim asked Fred, a local eccentric who kept a menagerie of pets such as ducks, geese, peacocks, a dozen varieties of chickens, raccoons, goats and sheep. Jim thought this was a pretty hopeless arrangement, because Mox hunted game and stray barnyard fowl that wandered within his territory. Nevertheless, Fred agreed to give it a try. But then his wife wouldn't allow Mox in the house. Fred solved the problem by putting Mox in the barn with the rest of the critters.

That night, Fred's wife asked, "Is he going to be all right? You'd better go check."

Dutifully, Fred made the trip and returned to report, "He's doing okay on the bed I made for him in the corner."

This didn't satisfy Dora. "Just for tonight, let's let him sleep on the porch."

Fred settled Mox on a bed of old blankets on the porch.

When Dora went to look at him an hour later, he looked so lonesome that she said, "Just for tonight, let's put his bed between ours."

A week later, Jim looked in on Mox. He was following Fred around the barnyard. Mox looked straight ahead and appeared oblivious to the delicious chicks and ducks that were underfoot. The mighty hunter submerged his instincts and became the guardian of what used to be food. As for his sleeping arrangements? He slept between Fred and Dora until he died of old age.

MY BEST POKER HAND

I covered my tray with a blanket, but it didn't help. The plane jerked and coffee burned me down the front. The pretty stewardess, now disheveled, struggled to gather trays and dishes as she squished through food in the aisle. The storm abated over Oklahoma, but a lady began filling a barf bag in explosive heaves. The smell of vomit, like sour garbage left in the sun, sent a sympathetic wave through the cabin. More bags came out.

We landed in sunny Dallas where the humidity clung near the saturation point; my clothes stuck to my sweaty body. I greeted Bill, a business associate who had come to pick me up. Did people live here by choice? I wondered.

As we checked in at the motel, 2-4-D filled the air. The clerk explained cheerfully, "that stuff kills everything."

"What does it do to people?" I muttered.

I showered and changed to join the others attending this national sales conference. I joined a poker game in progress. Hal, the boss, sucked away at his soggy cigar. The room was blue with smoke, but I barely noticed since I was polluting with king-sized Chesterfields.

Hal was the big winner so far. Though a little guy, he had a booming voice that irritated me. The other players worked for him so they either tolerated him or cowered under his abuses. The bully was taking the joy out of this wonderful game.

Nothing much happened until Hal got three deuces showing in five-card stud, nothing wild. He bet twenty dollars. Bill, with three clubs showing, called. I did also with my two fours and a jack showing. The dealer dealt us the last card. Hal got his fourth deuce, which was a miracle since there are only 624 of those in an entire deck. Bill got his four-card flush but Hal beat him with four deuces up. Hal looked at me with distaste as the dealer dropped a four on my hand, which curled from being squeezed too hard.

Hal blew a ring of smoke at each of his opponents and said, "$300 bucks on my four deuces." Bill raised $200 to make us believe that he had a straight flush, which would beat the four deuces.

He was missing the nine of clubs. I looked at my hole card, crunched a pretzel, washed down the salt with a slug of beer and called with, "Here's $500 and I raise another $200." I put a check for $700 on the pile of bills and change.

Hal's face flashed in disbelief and then flitted quickly back into a sneer as he blew one more ring at me. "You lying bastard, you ain't got diddly shit. I will call you both and raise one new Pontiac station wagon that's worth $3,000." He wrote a check for $400 to cover the raises and then wrote on his calling card, "My Station Wagon, worth $3,000." Then he signed it. He held the calling card aloft and dropped it slowly on the pile while he crunched his cigar and dribbled his ashes all over the money.

Bill dropped out because he needed one of two cards to make his straight flush, a nine or four of clubs. The nine fell earlier so the only winner was the four, which I claimed I had.

I said, "Hal, you'll lose your Pontiac with that bet. I'll let you take it back." He refused, so I wrote $3,000 on my calling card, signed it and put it on the pile. I then flipped over my four of clubs. His countenance changed from a sneer to disbelief and then to an ashen color. I tore his card in two and gave back his Pontiac. He said nothing as he accepted the torn card, stood up, and then shuffled off to his room.

SHARP LADIES

One of the most memorable encounters I had, occurred while listening to an erudite lecture on the political and religious history of Iran. I noticed a little lady I'd known for years, sitting next to me. She became tiny from advanced age, so she had to perch herself on the very edge of the bench we were sitting on. As the lecture went on, she appeared very well informed: when she disagreed, she muttered, "You've got that wrong," or nodded if she agreed.

The speaker droned on and he made a difficult subject more so by the excessive use of big, three-dollar words. When he used the word "exacerbate," it was more than I could handle. I nudged the lady with my elbow since she, too, looked bored and drowsy.

I said, "Hey, let's you and I exacerbate."

She peered over her glasses with smiling eyes and whispered, "Where? Your place or my place?"

I remember another remarkable woman. I met her at Phyllis Jordan's retirement party. Phyllis taught for forty years, and her friends organized the party at my house.

Many of Phyllis' teacher friends were invited. Some of them were retired for ten or fifteen years. I was standing next to an eighty-year-old. She was showing me pictures of her great-grandchildren. She kept dropping the pictures because her eyeglasses were falling down. I could see that one of the bows was missing. The little screw had dropped out, and she couldn't balance the glasses on her nose.

I remembered that I had an envelope full of little eyeglass screws in my desk drawer. I visualized putting in one of those screws to fix her glasses. I was sure she'd be pleased, so I asked laconically, "Would you like a screw?"

With a mischievous smile she answered with a throaty Marlene Dietrich voice, "Why, yes."

My third favorite lady was Amy. She was ninety-two years old, but looked and acted like a person thirty years younger. She kept in shape by swimming laps at the Northwest Tennis Club. Since she outlived all of her friends, her current friends were three to four decades younger. She was well known by the books she wrote, mostly outlandish stories about the days when she was a newspaper writer.

Once in a while she invited friends to her house for coffee. When she was ready to serve she asked, "And what inconsiderate son-of-a-bitch is going to ask for cream and sugar?"

Miraculously everyone wanted black coffee.

FISH STORIES

My passion for fishing defies logic. When I am out in the middle of a lake, it might be raining, the winds howling and the fish not biting. Why is this fun? It looks like masochism. Yet I am perfectly willing to undergo great hardship and expense just for this privilege. My rationalization is that I like the fuss of getting ready and of being with somebody compatible. The third reason is the exciting but intermittent reward of snagging a big one. For me, fishing is a socio-psychological sporting event.

I have fished with a number of different people but the most enjoyable was Johnny Johnson. His span of interest was similar to mine. We agreed on where to go and when to quit. Our fishing prowess and success were equally mediocre but he liked the sport even better than I did, if that is believable. On a particularly miserable day he said, "Only Johnny Johnson would put up with so much pain for so little." Though a great fishing buddy, he had two defects. First he was a hopeless Republican, which came from his snobbish Ivy League heritage. We solved this problem by not talking politics on our trips. The second was his wife, Jan, who didn't trust him and for a good reason. He was a philanderer. But he couldn't help it. He was born with the attributes, though invisible to me, which appealed to women. For example, while we were sitting in a corner of a noisy bar, away from the crowd and sipping beer, a woman came by to ask if she could join us. He chitchatted with her for a few minutes when she asked, "Would you like to join me at my table?" In deference to me he declined.

This scene with variations was repeated twice in a half an hour. With little imagination I could surmise what the next several steps could have been if I were not there. He didn't have to chase women. They came to him.

What made this guy so special? He was in his mid-thirties with ordinary good looks. He sported a small mustache, which always looked as though he had just trimmed it. He was not tall but he was a wiry athlete. Johnny had a liberal education from Penn State. He was well informed on world affairs, psychology, philosophy and sports. Occupationally, he was a star advertising salesman for a newspaper, a polished conversationalist and especially gifted in the power of persuasion.

To his wife, Johnny's gift was a burden. To curb some of his after-hours activities, Jan put a very short chain on him, which she jerked often with screeching sarcasm. Actually, this was poor psychology. He resented his confinement, not only because of his truncated social life, but, most devastating of all, he wasn't allowed to go fishing. The result was that neither of them was happy.

I needed a new fishing buddy as my old one moved away. Johnny proved to be perfect, so through a wonderful turn of events for him, Jan trusted me. She calibrated me as a wholesome type who didn't hang around bars chasing women and therefore would keep Johnny away from all temptations. Now, whenever Johnny wanted to go fishing, I'd get a fishing pass for him by asking Jan, "Can Johnny come out to play with me?" Jan always approved. The Romeo was in fish heaven! We were able to fish often all over Minnesota and Wisconsin.

Once while fishing on Lake Cornelia near St. Paul, a powerboat thundered past us and almost overturned our canoe. After cursing the idiot, I noticed something splashing in the wake of the big boat. It was a Northern Pike hit by the intruder. Johnny lifted out a thirteen and one half-pound lunker that was thirty-eight inches long. We spent the afternoon pulling it out of the water just to admire the immensity of the fish.

We went to a local bar to celebrate the unusual catch. A number of people in the bar came to see our fish, which we had stretched out in its full glory under the hood of my VW bug. We explained nothing and listened to the people surmising what it must have felt like catching something that big.

We celebrated so much that we didn't get home until four in the morning. My wife wouldn't let me in the house so we went to Johnny's. When Jan saw the fish, she said, "I can understand why you guys were celebrating. You've never caught anything of consequence." Johnny expanded the lie by explaining what a struggle it was to bring in that fish. I too became a liar by being silent.

That fish gained fame among our friends. With each telling, the fish grew bigger: the latest version after three years was that we caught a state record Northern. At a large party, Johnny had one too many Fisherman's Punch and confessed to everyone that we had lied. He explained how we really caught the fish. By association, I was a fallen angel. I was sure that Jan would write me off and put an end to our fishing trips. Instead, she forgave me. "Carl," she said, "that fish story is so wholesome compared to Johnny's women chasing, I thought it was fun."

FISHING BUDDIES

Matt and I played doubles tennis every Monday. He overwhelmed opponents, not with skill, but by his impatience and will to win. When he served, he didn't waste a minute. If his first serve failed, the second serve was on the way before the first had quit bouncing.

John Taylor, though an accomplished tennis player, wilted when he faced the Matt Sutton wall. Though only about five-six, as a college student, Matt played first-string quarterback for the University of Minnesota. With a Ph.D. in aeronautical engineering from Ohio State and high capabilities, he rose to a senior executive position in the company. Though impatient and demanding, the people in his organization loved the man for his integrity and his skills in running very successful organizations.

Matt asked me to join his fishing party as he drove me home from the tennis courts. Interspersed with his invitation, he directed the traffic by cursing every driver around.

"Hey, lady, let's get that gol-darned car going. The light has changed." Actually, only a microsecond elapsed since the light flipped from red to green.

I accepted the invitation to go fishing before he finished asking the question, for this was an honor. This fishing party had not changed its membership for about twenty years. I heard that someone had to die before anybody else was invited. Indeed, this appeared to be true, for the opening was created by a member's death the previous year leaving only five active members.

Matt organized this fishing group, which specialized in catching walleyes in the Canadian Boundary Waters. The group took two boats, each with a high-powered motor. The style was to roar twenty miles away into the wilderness, far from crowded water.

Fishing with Matt was exciting, because he knew where the fish were. The bad news was he fished with the same impatience he exercised when driving. Once, while parked in the middle of the Lake of the Woods, we discussed where to move for better fishing. With his engine idling at a high roar, he shouted, "Let's go to Astron Bay," and threw his 100-horse Johnson into full throttle and shot off to the right.

His trolling ten-horse, tilted high, crashed over our boat scraping off everything, including our windshield.

Unaware of the calamity, he made a wide turn to complete his devastation. At fifty miles an hour, he skimmed over a bed of boulders submerged about a foot. This dented the bottom of his brand-new boat and wrecked the entire bottom half of his outboard.

In our fishing party of six, there were three malcontents who spent a lot of time complaining about the food we had on our trips. They neither wanted to cook nor did they know how to, yet they kept up a chorus of complaints like spoiled children. They'd say, "Ham? I hate that stuff." Or, "These damned fried potatoes still have skins on them." Pete, who took on the job of buying and cooking most of the food, complained back, "I don't know how to cook to satisfy you damn guys."

One night, during happy hour, I told them the story about four hunters and a cook. The cook of the hunting party shared Pete's problem. One day, while the unhappy cook was walking around in the wilderness, he saw a fresh mound of moose dung. With a flash of insight into how to solve his problem, he scooped up the pile and took it back to the cabin. He made a beautiful moose dung pie for his colleagues.

When the tired but happy hunters returned, the cook announced that, henceforth, if anyone bitched about the food, he would become the next cook. Then he set his trap.

After a glorious meal, the cook served the pie. One hunter took a bite and spit it out. "This is moose shit!" he exclaimed. Then, with barely a break in the sentence, he continued, "but it's *good.*"

Later on, after telling this same story to our spoiled children, I announced that we would initiate the same policy about who would be the next cook. The bitching stopped, but after each meal we had to listen to the chorus, "This is shit, but it's good shit."

Adolf Bostrom, nicknamed "Ozzie," was a klutz fisherman. His equipment was a disgrace—the pole was a steel rod, the reel was a cast iron monstrosity, and his line was a nylon rope. I think he must have bought his equipment at a war surplus store in the forties.

At the fishing-business-end, there was a marvel of concatenated hardware: a steel line, a sinker, swivels, and a lure with a minnow impaled on its hook. What fish would snap at this offering? Once in a while, a demented fish would get tangled in his line or impale itself on his hook. Ozzie caught about one-fifth as much as the rest of us, but he showed not the slightest inclination to change his fishing style.

One day Ozzie made a mighty cast, missing Dave's head by a couple of microns. The reel whirred, the lure dropped into the lake, but the reel kept spinning. This led to two disasters: a snarled line and a lure snagged at the bottom of the lake. "God," he moaned, "that's my fancy Daredevil that I just bought."

To save the lure, Dave began pulling the cord that started the engine. The line was taut as the boat began to drift. There was no danger of the line breaking, because Ozzie used a fifty pound test line, though he never caught anything weighing more than a couple of pounds. Dave eased the boat over the lure. Oz hoisted a submerged tree as well as his lure. He spent the rest of the afternoon unraveling his line.

The amazing thing about Ozzie was, though his equipment was marginal and his fishing style incompetent, he was the greatest engineer I ever knew. He kept sharp by figuring out how mechanical gadgets worked and how they could be made. He liked tinkering with machines so much that he rejoiced when they broke down. He was a gem on these fishing trips. He would fix the cars and boat engines when they quit working. In these situations, he transformed from a fumbling fisherman to a serious, mechanical genius. He listened to the noises the machine made, touched a few things and sometimes he tasted what oozed out. He whipped out his tools and became a blur of activity. If something was broken, he made the part.

Ozzie was the company's most prolific inventor with about one hundred patents. One big money maker was his piezoelectric lighter used for igniting the burner of gas water heaters. This device was also the igniter for cigarette lighters sold around the world.

Though his fishing trip was costing him three or four hundred dollars, Ozzie wasn't there to fish. He made it a social event, telling us outlandish stories about his experiences.

One night he told us that Bebe Shoppe, a beauty from our small town of Hopkins, Minnesota, had been Miss America in 1948. She was a big girl and was probably the most wholesome Miss America of all time. She played the vibraharp. Ozzie saw a twice-life sized picture of Bebe at a local shopping center. He reported to us, "Here was Miss America, the perfection of womanhood, and she had corns." I moaned, "Ozzie, you dumb bastard. Who cares about her lousy corns? You're looking at the wrong things. Look higher up and savor the rest of her loveliness." No wonder he never married.

One day, Ozzie noticed a five-gallon milk jug without its cover. Looking inside, he saw a hundred flies sucking up the little bit of milk the farmer hadn't poured out. He put the cover back on, shook the can, and drowned the flies and left the can uncovered. A half-hour later, he returned to the can and found one hundred more happy flies sucking milk without even wondering why their comrades were dead. Ozzie put the cover back on and drowned the second batch. He did this a few more times to amass 500 drowned flies. He poured his catch and the residual milk into a bowl and gave them to the chickens. He chuckled, "Those chickens love the protein."

When Ozzie went to the State Fair in St. Paul, he watched a piglet eating slop out of a trough while urinating and defecating. When it oinked, everything stopped. He observed, "What a marvel of detailed balance! Stuff was going into the efficient animal with stuff coming out. The residual difference became pork."

FISHING WITH WARREN

Warren Wilde must rank as the greatest expert alive on the Small Mouth Bass. He specialized in this species because they put up such a vigorous fight. They had no other redeeming qualities since they were small, bony and not particularly tasty.

Every July, Warren and I met for a week of fishing by going to a family camp on Star Island, a four-pointed star in the center of Cass Lake in northern Minnesota. Within the boundary of the island nestles another lake: it's called Lake Windigo and covers 1,100-acres with neither a river nor a stream connected to the big lake. The uniqueness of a large lake within an island captured the attention of Robert Ripley, who featured Lake Windigo in his cartoon, *Believe It Or Not*.

Windigo had little fishing pressure because it required a portage of about one hundred yards through a small trail infested with vicious mosquitoes. From our camp, we rowed a canoe to the entry of the trail, portaged the canoe and all our fishing gear and canoed onto Lake Windigo. Warren knew the lake so well he identified his fishing spot by a certain patch of reeds that poked out of the water. When we approached the magic cache of fish, he guided me with precise directions, "Go forward and to the left ten yards. Whoa, back up two feet. Drop the anchor six inches out on the left side."

When we dropped our lines, we got strikes immediately. We hauled in perches, crappies, northern pikes, walleyes, rock basses, large mouth basses and Warren's specialty, the small mouth bass. When we had a stringer of about twenty fishes, Warren hooked onto a big one. After a struggle, he landed the biggest small mouth he caught in his thirty-year quest for a lunker of that specie. He admired his prize for a few minutes and concluded, "I've got to take this into Cass Lake to have it mounted. I want it to be alive when I give it to the taxidermist." Being a good fishing buddy, I agreed to help him. We portaged the canoe with all the gear through that miserable trail and rowed five miles into Cass Lake. We took his monster to the taxidermist who agreed it was an award-winner.

We drove back to our canoe, rowed five miles to Lake Windigo, portaged the canoe again while getting a hundred mosquito bites. The insects didn't bite Warren because his blood was rotten and not luscious like mine. We dropped anchor at the exact spot specified by the expert. We caught a variety of fish with no effort. Then, it happened again. Warren brought in a small mouth that he thought was even bigger than the last one. The bastard wanted to take this one into Cass Lake to have it mounted instead of the other one. I went along with his folly and made the second round trip, The fish taxidermist said, "Since I've already started on the other one, I'll have to charge you for it." Our small mouth expert paid for two trophies.

When we got back to Warren's hole, he yelped, "I forgot to tell him I wanted the two basses pointed nose to nose and not swimming in the same direction." He pleaded for a third round trip. This time I held my ground and refused to help him. I told him he could find out what happened next week on our way home. Besides he was wrecking my vacation.

That hole seemed to teem with fish because we kept dragging them out as though the source had an infinite population. Lucky for me, Warren's small mouth catches remained normal-sized. We had enough fish to stage a fish fry for the entire camp twice.

On the way home, we stopped to see what the taxidermist did. He had them swimming in the same direction. Though Warren's fish were record breakers, he still looked gloomy. I gave him cheerful counsel: "Go catch the other monster in Windigo and then supervise the taxidermist very carefully lest you end up with three going the same way."

FISHING WITH WARREN

(A Sestina[2])

Minnesota, home of Chippewas, giant mosquitoes
And 10,000 lakes almost devoid of fish.
The sleepy town of Cass Lake is on the south shore
Of Cass Lake. Within this lake is star-shaped Star Island.
Contained within this isle is 1100-acre Lake Windigo,
So unusual, Ripley's "Believe it or not," featured this lake.

It took fifty rods by portage from Cass Lake to the little lake
Through overgrown brush and fierce female mosquitoes.
After 100 bites from these state birds, we reach Windigo
Which, unlike the fishless Cass Lake, does have some fish,
A secret kept honor-bound by all residents of Star Island.
It's safe because Windigo is invisible from Cass' shore.

Warren Wilde, guided me on Windigo toward the far shore,
To a clump of reeds sticking inches out of the Lake,
To the fish hole unknown to cabin owners of Star Island.
We dropped out lines while fighting pesky mosquitoes,
Then wham! He hooked the Small Mouth Bass fish.
Wilde caught his largest in twenty years of fishing Windigo.

"To the taxidermist," he directed. "Portage out of Windigo."
We J-stroked our canoe five miles to Cass' far shore
And delivered his record lunker of that specie of fish
To the taxidermist and then paddled toward our tiny lake.
We portaged and stumbled while slapping mosquitoes
And back toward our secret hole, the best on Star Island.

We went to the most sacred place on the island.
Then bang! Warren caught an even bigger bass in Windigo
"To the taxidermist." "Give more blood to mosquitoes?"
We paddled wearily back to the lake's far shore,
Delivered the monster fish and returned across the lake.
Now Warren had two big bills for his blasted fish.

Back at our hole, Warren brooded about his last fish.
He jumped up and demanded, "We must leave this island."

I want the basses facing each other. Let's go back."
"You're out of your mind. We're not leaving Windigo,"
I shouted as the sun sank out of sight.
We caught a stringer, went ashore.

My vacation ruined by his folly,
Forced to paddle and fight mosquitoes
On Saturday, with aching arms and mosquito welts,
We returned to see what he'd done with Warren's fish.
Both basses pointed east.
He swore, "The hell with Cass Lake."

CHAPTER VIII

Career

PHYSICS

Meanwhile, I was working hard on my studies. The welcome I received at the Institute of Technology was particularly heartwarming. Friendships that were to last a lifetime were initiated. And the members of the department faculty went out of their way to be helpful. During my first week on campus, Dr. Clifford N. Wall, then professor of physics, invited me to his home for dinner.

Dr. William G. Shepherd even went so far as to offer to lend me money when my wife, baby, and I were living on $111 a month. He became my advisor, and was always there when I needed him.

I also appreciated the wonderful support and encouragement of Dr. Edward L. Hill, professor of theoretical physics.

DR. EDWARD L. HILL

Minneapolis, Minnesota

I had the extreme good fortune to have had five teachers that helped

me shape my life and career. One was a neighbor, two were high
school teachers and two, university professors—Dr. W. G. Shepherd and Dr. Edward L. Hill. Dr. Hill had the most profound
influence. He instilled in me a love of theoretical physics. I took
almost every math course offered at the University. And I eventually received a Ph.D., specializing in the physics of the solid state.
This combination of fields resulted in my having the pleasurable
occupation of massaging numbers and equations all day long and
getting paid for what seemed like play to me.

Dr. Hill was short, in his mid-forties when I met him in 1946,
he had a few wisps of hair that he combed back with care and his
eyes twinkled through his rimless glasses. He wrote equations on
the blackboard with great care, especially the upper case sigma
that meant "the summation of . . ." He loved Latin expressions
such as *mutatis mutandis* and *sua sponte*.

Early in the term, he broke his right arm but continued to
lecture by writing on the blackboard with his left hand. By the
time he had his cast removed three months later, he had become
so agile that he began writing with a chalk in each hand. With his
newly developed dexterity, if the chalk were on his left, he'd write
with his left and with his right hand if the chalk happened to be
on the other side. His lectures now moved along briskly because
he drew graphs with both hands.

Because he was competent in both math and physics, he was
a full professor in both the physics and the pure math depart-
ments. He was the most admired teacher in the department, but
unfortunately, he taught only graduate courses so most of the students didn't know him. What an asset he could have been if he
had taught freshman physics, the course that went over most students' heads. Enrico Fermi of the University of Chicago and Richard Feynman of Cal Tech, both Nobel Laureates taught the
freshman courses, by their request. The latter even wrote texts for

the freshman class.

Dr. Hill had the talent for making difficult subjects seem easy. An example was the eloquence with which he explained the properties of spaces with an infinite number of dimensions in his course on the Mathematical Foundation of Quantum Mechanics. I left his lectures feeling that I understood every bit. He always typed his notes and kept a copy in the physics library. There was so much competition for reading his notes that a committee of classmates took turns copying them for duplication for all that wanted them. I think it was his meticulous preparation that made his lectures so successful.

I perused the lecture notes before and after classes. The former reading enabled me to write down points that were not clear and the latter reading implanted the subject solidly into my head. I took every course he taught and I often said, "I would take Hill's course even if it were Sanskrit for I was confident that he would make the materials understandable."

In sharp contrast, I took a course in advanced electrodynamics, an easier subject, from a different professor. His lectures were so difficult to understand that, from a class that began with twenty-five students, it dwindled down to three by the end of the year. The others either quit or audited the course for fear that they might get a bad grade. I hung in to the bitter end, learned practically nothing but got straight A's, evidently for my tenacity.

You'd think there is little humor or happiness in theoretical physics, but Professor Hill smiled often and joked now and then. It was comfortable being there for there was no stress and it was easy to take understandable and legible notes. I had wonderful discussions with him in his office when he was my advisor for my master's degree. He took the trouble to explain things to me even if they had nothing to do with his courses.

In September 1947, I took Hill's course entitled, *Physics of the*

Solid State. By coincidence, a solid-state device called the transistor was invented on December 23, 1947. Though I didn't know about this event when I took his course, solid-state physics was destined to become the basis of my profession in industry.

In 1949 when I was about to begin working on my dissertation for a Ph.D., Dr. Hill agreed to be my advisor. The plan was to master quantum mechanics, electrodynamics and special relativity and then develop a thesis from these three subjects. But I had no means of support since I had used up the G. I. Bill from both the U.S. Government and the State of California. In addition I was too late to apply for either a teaching or research assistantship. I was in a quandary because I now had a wife and a one-year old baby. By luck, Dr. Shepherd, who taught static and dynamic electricity liked the way I solved problems in his class so he offered me a research assistantship if I would switch my dissertation subject to solid state physics and be his Ph.D. candidate. I accepted his offer with some misgivings because I hated to give up quantum electrodynamics.

Twenty-five years later, I wrote Professor Hill a letter thanking him for his mentoring. I mentioned how valuable his lectures were to me and that the only notes I kept after nine years of college were from his courses. I added that he inspired me to be a theoretical physicist like him, but that was not to be because that took more talent than I had. The letter took about a month to reach him because he had just retired and traveled before settling down in La Jolla, California. He reminisced and mentioned that we had met at his mid-career. Three months later, I read that he died from a massive heart attack. As a final tribute, I read his Ph.D. dissertation on electron spin that I checked out from the library of the University of Minnesota.

HONEYWELL CORPORATE RESEARCH CENTER

Finally, at age thirty, I received my Ph.D. I then proposed to Louise that I stay for one more year. I wanted a Ph.D. in math because I liked that subject better than physics—it was the math part of physics I enjoyed. I had all the course work done so all I needed was a dissertation. My chosen topic was "Non-linear Differential Equations." Louise shot me down with, "Carl, you're a big boy now. You have to go to work."

I went to work, but during the next forty-five years I wondered what my life would have been as a mathematician and a university professor. I'm pretty sure that I would have ended in a field such as Chaos Theory.

I went to work at Honeywell under false pretenses. I planned to work only three months or so during the summer until Lou had our fourth child. Then I planned to move to a job waiting for me at Bell Labs, the greatest lab in the world where the prospects of learning something were unparalleled. But one thing led to another, and before I knew it, I stayed for thirty-three years. Indeed, I had hired for life.

Dr. Van Bearinger hired me as a Research Physicist at the Honeywell Corporate Research Center in Minneapolis. My responsibility was to produce research results of the quality that would be publishable in prestigious journals such as *The Physical Review*. I wondered what the benefit would be to Honeywell for such work. The company didn't seem big enough to afford the luxury of basic research. Nonetheless, my work was play, since I would have done that kind of work for nothing.

Some of the most capable people were the technicians, and many of them were older than the scientists. Elmer Christensen was a technician who helped me with my experiments. He had the uncanny talent of sensing what I needed before I asked for it. On one occasion, I murmured, "I wish I could display this data as the logarithm of current versus time."

Fifteen minutes later he led me to an oscilloscope and said, "Is this what you wanted?"

"Yep, exactly."

Another ace was Don, a former Navy electronics technician, who knew how to do everything—though, like Elmer, he had no formal scientific training. When we had coffee breaks, he was the star of the show because he told outlandish stories. Through sheer brilliance this man was promoted to the level of an engineer and topped his career by winning the most prestigious engineer/scientist award offered by the company, the Sweatt Award.

After three months of work, Ed Rexer, my supervisor, came around to tell me that I was getting a fifty-dollar a month raise.

"What for?" I asked. "I haven't done anything yet."

A couple of months later, Ed came around again with another raise and said, "I've promoted you to Research Supervisor."

What a shock! Never in my life did I ever plan or expect to be in management. Why was this happening? I still hadn't done anything of consequence, yet I was in charge of several scientists, engineers, technicians, lab aids and a secretary.

I shared an office with Allen Nussbaum, a recent Ph.D. from the University of Pennsylvania. Since I was in the office most of the time and he worked in the lab, I answered many of his phone calls. One frequent caller was his wife, Barbara. She would say, "Tell Allen to bring home bread." At other times she would give me a long shopping list, which had some surprising items such as a size thirty-four bra with a "B" cup.

One day, when Barbara called, I thought of a devilish prank. I used a hoarse voice and said, "I'm sorry, but Allen isn't here. He's having a late lunch with his wife." Then I promptly hung up.

The next morning, a ruffled Allen with blood shot eyes confronted me with, "You rotten, lousy bastard. Are you trying to break up my marriage? You have to go home with me and confess to Barbara, or I'm going to truncate you." Forty-five years have slipped by, but Barbara and Allen are still two of my best friends.

After attending a few more administration meetings, I decided that this was a most boring way to make a living. At a Research Center's Vice President's meeting, the boss passed out a few memos that were stamped *Confidential.* I perused them and found nothing that seemed very secret. Unconsciously, I tore one sheet into a square and began folding an origami stork. Pretty soon I had two. At the time of a particularly long-winded meeting, I had amassed a total of seventeen storks and lined them up in front of me. Subsequently, I referred to it as the "seventeen-stork meeting." The boss began shooting arrows of displeasure, so I quit my art and behaved like the other good supervisors.

I began a campaign to get rid of the supervisory job. It took a year, but the boss relented and made me a Staff Physicist with the responsibility of doing good basic research. Then I was back in heaven.

PURE AND APPLIED RESEARCH

John Blakemore became my working associate. He was a genius who had earned his Ph.D. at twenty-three from Queen Mary College in London. This man could multiply big numbers in his head and solve quadratic equations with a slide rule. He had the gift of figuring out what the electrons were doing just by looking at the plot of the data.

We always argued for a long time before starting a project. He would say, "But, Cahl, you cahn't do that." Though I was tempted to mimic his British accent and say, "But John, you cahn," I never did. Once we agreed on an approach, we rolled ahead with teamwork and proficiency. We got so that we could crank out a paper every few weeks. Those years with Dr. Blakemore were the best of my working life and I would have been happy doing research for the rest of my working career.

We wrote a proposal to the Signal Corps on the study of the electrical, optical, magnetic and crystalline properties of Tellurium, one of the six semiconductor elements that exist in nature. Tom Davies, a talented technician, who worked for me, grew a single crystal of Tellurium by the Czochralski method. Concurrently, I developed equipment for purifying Te. By zone refining continuously for several weeks, I obtained Te that was 99.999999% pure starting with ingots that were only 95% pure. Now by growing single crystals from these purified materials, we were able to study the intrinsic properties of this semiconductor. Nobody else in the world had Te as pure and perfect as ours.

Though basic research in Te seemed sterile, it had a fall-out in useful technology and products. I developed the process for making crystals that worked as infrared sensors. The technology was transferred to Honeywell's Radiation division where the mercury-cadmium-telluride sensors and systems became its main business. I noticed that these sensors were used in the Desert Storm War.

I had an idea for making defect free crystals, but I had to abandon that work because management transferred me. This was the second of the three work related disappointments I had. The first was not getting a Ph.D. in math, the second, not making defect free crystals and the third was not accepting Dr. William Shockley's offer to be his Materials Manager for his newly formed company. Shockley won the Nobel Prize jointly with John Bardeen and John Brattain. I kissed off the opportunity to be at the ground floor of the Silicon Valley explosion. I could have become very wealthy, but instead I remained a pauper by staying at Honeywell.

THE SEMICONDUCTOR DIVISION

Rivera Beach, Florida (1960)

Although I didn't know him at the time, Stephen F. Keating was promoted to Executive Vice President and a member of the Board of Directors. Apparently, at his first board meeting, he asked, "Why is the Semiconductor division losing money month after month?"

The chairman replied, "I don't know. That's why you are in charge of that division. Find out what's wrong and then fix it."

Steve Keating may have left the meeting wondering what a semiconductor was, because a few days later Mrs. Keating sent me a note asking that question. I sent her a note and a picture of an orchestra conductor cut in half.

To solve his problem, Steve Keating hired Dr. Tex Holt, Professor of Physics at Harvard University at a rumored consulting fee of $ 10,000 per week, which was very large in 1960. His specialty was physics of the gaseous state and not the solid state, but that was close enough for the task at hand.

Tex checked out the management staff of the Semiconductor division and then roamed around the company interviewing many people. I was one of them. Tex interrogated me for a couple of hours, looking for what I thought were things wrong with the division. He took voluminous notes in Gregg shorthand on three by five cards. He then disappeared and I promptly forgot about him and went back to my research on perfect mercury-cadmium-telluride crystals.

About a week later, I received a phone call from Steve Keating. He asked me to come to his office on the sixth floor of the general office building. When his secretary showed me into his office, I thought he must be a big wheel—his rug was so deep I stumbled as I walked across the room. He was a tall, friendly man with steel-gray hair that formed a cowlick near his part. He told me the results of Tex Holt's investigation and enumerated some of the recommendations he had made. I remembered three of them:

"(1) The division is fixable, but it would be okay to sell the division off because its products are obsolete.

"(2) It needed more people who were knowledgeable in the semiconductor technology.

"(3) Send Nomura to Riviera Beach, Florida, to fix that operation."

I don't remember the other suggestions.

Steve concluded with, "Go to Riviera Beach as the technical director in charge of engineering, production, quality control, administration and personnel. When you get there, terminate one third of the employees and then fix whatever is wrong."

This was an abrupt change for an amoral scientist whose only experience was managing research projects—a country club job with no profit and loss responsibilities. I, moreover, was to begin this new assignment by being a hatchet man. I thought about the proposal for a couple of days and decided to take it. I knew then that I would have to kiss off research and do serious and difficult management.

After arriving at the Riviera Beach facility, I called in all the department managers and told them to totem pole every employee and then draw a line under the top 67 percent, but not to terminate anyone until I saw the total roster. I wanted the option of shuffling names first.

Some of the managers came in to suggest that I keep Elsie Smith because "she was the best," or to keep Bob "because he's the only one who knows how to operate those diffusion furnaces." I made some changes, then told all the managers to terminate those below the line. The next day, I made the headlines as the hatchet man who had swooped down from Minneapolis.

Honeywell's Chairman and CEO knew I was a green-as-grass manager, so he sent Mr. Phil Jacobson, his administrative assistant, to be my mentor. Phil was sixty-four years old, and a bachelor. He had been a senior executive in the early days of the company. His primary job for many years was to track the *Fortune 500*. He did this by buying one share of every stock to get their annual reports. When we wandered down Worth Avenue in Palm Beach, he would recite which company merged with which; who the CEO was; plus an account of the company's financial data, stock performance and other details.

"With your encyclopedic memory of info, you should be rich," I mused.

"I don't own one share of stock," he replied. "I have been managing my unmarried sister's stock portfolio for about thirty years, so she's very wealthy."

I was extremely busy, so I learned very quickly not to ask Phil questions during the working hours because he was apt to burn up my day answering my question. I saved questions such as, "Why do we need the quality control department?" for dinner. Phil would orate for about three hours. Through these nightly lessons I learned a great deal about management, even details such as how to count parts without errors.

Being a conservative Catholic who spent his entire life immersed with the concerns of the company, he was totally unschooled in street talk and experience with the marvels of women. Thus, I kidded him unmercifully. For example, one time he came rushing into my office to announce, "Two secretaries didn't show up for work. What are we going to do?"

I seized the opportunity. "Don't worry, Phil. I've sent in an order for two overload secretaries. The two absent ones have the crud."

In total innocence he'd walk into my trap and ask, "What's crud?"

"Everything they eat turns into shit."

He'd wander away shaking his head. No doubt, some of this went back to corporate headquarters.

Cape Canaveral was about seventy miles up the road from us. When NASA announced it was about to make its first space shot, I told the employees they could watch the shot from the windows.

Phil blanched. "Now you've set a precedent for watching every space shot that comes along."

"This is a once-in-a-lifetime event," I replied. "Why not give them five minutes? It might do wonders for productivity."

And it did, for this was a show most people in the world could see only on TV. Our employees saw it in the flesh.

By now the employees were settled in their jobs and had forgotten about the layoff. I learned the names of the factory workers, most of whom were women. Once, while kidding them during their coffee breaks, I referred to myself as the "inscrutable oriental." This remark produced howling laughter. They practically rolled around on the floor. I didn't think it was that funny, especially since I'd stolen it from James Thurber. Later, a woman came to see me in my office to explain why there was so much laughter. They thought I'd said "unscrewable oriental."

When he thought he had educated me enough, Phil went back to Minneapolis and told the chairman, "I don't want a promotion or a raise. I just want to keep doing what I am doing now and retire at the end of the year." His maiden sister died shortly after he retired and he inherited her large estate. He also married and vanished from my radar screen.

POWER TRANSISTORS

In the meantime, the division had little to sell because the products were alloyed germanium power transistors. These were at the end of their product life and were being phased out by many of our customers. My solution was to develop and produce a family of modern transistors made by the planar process on epitaxially grown silicon on silicon wafers, but we didn't have the technology or the engineers. Jim McKeen, the personnel manager, gave Bryan Page the job of recruiting the experts. We told him to go to Motorola or TI to look for engineers who knew the epitaxial deposition process.

He tore out of the room shouting, "Planar-epitaxial layers— Motorola—Texas Instruments." Five minutes later, he returned and asked, "Where's Motorola?"

I thought that if this man had a plan, he could own the earth with his unbounded energy and enthusiasm. Bryan found the engineers we needed and we went to work.

We were in a technology that advanced so rapidly that products became obsolete in two years. We therefore, concocted a strategy for products with a long life. We focused on silicon power transistors, which would be used in power supplies. No matter how quickly other products were supplanted with newer devices, power transistors will always be needed. Our planar epitaxials would meet that need. Thus we developed a family of transistors with current carrying capacities of two, five, ten and twenty amperes.

Our customers liked them but were slow in changing to a new technology. Honeywell's management, in the meantime, became impatient and decided to sell the division.

Honeywell found a buyer easily. The stock of the buying company was about thirty-five dollars a share. After selling the division, the big order we were waiting for came in. But the new company shipped the inventory we produced for enough revenue to pay for the division. Their stocks, accordingly, soared. The employees who were unhappy about being sold with the company suddenly grew happy: they were sporting Cadillacs. It was a mistake selling this division. Thirty years later, our planar epitaxial transistors were still being sold just as we developed them.

THE SOLID STATE ELECTRONICS CENTER

The new Chairman, Jim Binger, asked me to return to Minneapolis to organize a new center called SSEC (Solid State Electronic Center). My objective was to develop the underlying integrated circuit technology and then persuade the company's divisions to convert their products from obsolete vacuum tubes and electromechanical technologies to modern solid state. This was a tough assignment because the divisions didn't want to spend money and degrade their earnings. It also was tough getting approvals for such projects. My job was to give them enemas because it was good for them.

Since selling from the bottom up was an almost hopeless task, I went from the top down. I developed a presentation that described the technology, its possible applications, expected improved performance, higher reliability and lower costs. The bottom line of the pitch was that if we didn't do it, our competitors would, leaving us behind. I presented this story to the chairman and his staff and then to the president and his staff, to the executive vice presidents and their staffs and down through all levels of management. Now engineering and marketing managers had little trouble getting approvals for new product and product upgrade requests. Their bosses were waiting to approve these requests.

Our first shot at a high volume product was the Hall Sensor, a device based on an effect discovered by Professor Hall of Johns Hopkins near the turn of the century. Two engineers, Ev Vorthmann and Joe Maupin, developed the Hall chip. I took the idea to the MicroSwitch division in Freeport, Illinois. Harry Meyer, the Director of Engineering demanded, "How can you guarantee me that the product will work for computer keyboards." Nothing I said satisfied Harry. In desperation, I laid my life on the line with, "If the Hall Sensor does not work, I'll come back here with my sword and I'll fall on it."

This pleased Harry. He said, "Agreed. Let's do it and let the chips fall where they may."

The Hall Sensor was a huge success for keyboards. It continued its success by replacing the breaker and condenser in the distributor. These became the standard in most cars made in the U.S. and Europe. The Japanese automakers produced their own Hall Sensors and did not buy one from us. We made billions of them and the product had a life of thirty-five years.

The second most profitable product was the *autofocus* opto-electronics for single reflex cameras. This wonderful invention was the brainchild of Norm Stauffer, who worked in the photo-electronics unit. The device was a complicated silicon opto-electronic integrated circuit, and it was extremely hard to produce. It soon became clear that we'd have to overrun by about 1.5 million dollars.

So I prepared a one-slide presentation to the Chairman of the Board, asking that I be allowed to spend the extra amount. The title of that one slide was "Dancing Bear." I concluded the pitch with, "When you dance with a bear, you can't quit just because you are tired. Please approve my request."

Though senior management tend to be almost humorless, Mr. Spencer laughed and said, "Go ahead."

In time we did get that device into production and supplied a few camera makers in Japan.

In the meantime, I was preparing to retire. But before doing so, I had an assignment in Japan. I was to consult with Yamatake-Honeywell, a company 50 percent owned by Honeywell.

While in Japan, I met a retired vice president of a company that made cameras. I was introduced to him as a Yamatake person. Not realizing my connection with the *autofocus* device, this man boasted, "I spent $12 million trying to reproduce that Honeywell device but failed. My successor did succeed in copying the device."

The next day I flew back to Minneapolis and received approval from management to sue the Japanese company for infringing on our *autofocus* patents.

Our legal department went to work on the suit. I then retired, but about a year later I heard that Honeywell was laying-off employees from Corporate Headquarters. I wrote to the CEO and urged him not to lay off the lawyers who were working on the *autofocus* suit. He assured me that there would be no cutbacks on that project. It took about six years and $12 million of legal fees, but Honeywell won its patent infringement suit from twelve Japanese camera companies. The proceeds were about $400 million, a very good return on our investment.

It took fifteen years to meet our objectives. In the meantime, SSEC grew from annual revenues of $40,000 to annual revenues of $160,000,000. It also became SSED, a division of the company. The company promoted me several times.

VHSIC (VERY HIGH SPEED
INTEGRATED CIRCUITS)

In 1981, the five major electronics companies in Japan announced they had organized a joint venture to develop the most advanced integrated circuit technology in the world to build the fifth generation computer. This shocked the U.S., especially the Department of Defense, because for national security reasons, America must maintain its superiority in technology. To have Japan surpass us was unthinkable, especially since integrated circuits (IC) were an American invention.

The Department of Defense (DoD) quickly received approval to spend a few hundred million dollars to push the U.S. semiconductor industry ahead of Japan. All U.S. electronics companies were invited to submit proposals, first for Phase I and later for Phase II, which would guarantee us international leadership. About fifteen to twenty companies bid, mostly as partners of large companies such as Intel and IBM. Honeywell chose to bid alone. About eight contracts were let, one of them to us, and the race was on with each team designing and producing working models of the world's most complex circuits. These chips were probably of the complexity of a Pentium chip.

We chose a computer type chip that processed optically scanned data. Our objective was to make a design that was error free, a feat no one had accomplished to date. This was exceedingly important because it took about three months to process these devices. Thus, each faulty design burned up $250,000 and three months. On our first design, the printout of errors made a stack about four inches thick. A second pass reduced the pile to about ten pages. On the fourth try, we registered no errors. When we processed the design, we got the world's first pass success for a VHSIC level of complexity.

We were so pleased about being the first in the nation to pull off this feat, I bought a full page ad in the *Wall Street Journal* that said: "We did it, the world's first, first-pass success." I ran the ad to recognize the design team for its achievement, to attract the best engineers in the country, and to be sure we'd be an early winner of Phase II and with a high price tag. This ad was worth $50,000 to me because it is not often that you hit a home run.

CONSULTANCY

It turned out that I enjoyed management—I could still participate in the technical decisions, but I also liked the challenge of getting people to work well together. I continued in management and retired in 1986 as a Corporate Senior Vice President.

But before retiring, I had one final special assignment. I was asked to figure out what to do with a company Honeywell owned that was losing about $300,000 a day. I became President of this failing company. It couldn't make integrated circuit products cost-effective. It produced a product that cost $6.50 to make, but it sold it for only $1.25. Fixing the company was too costly and it would take too long so I undertook the task of shutting down. I had three top priorities:

  1. To fill the outstanding orders so that we didn't

leave the customers stranded.
2. To find jobs for the displaced employees.
3. To sell off all the assets at a minimum loss.

We filled every order and for some customers, we made extra products that were not available anywhere else. For jobs, we set up a job fair and invited all of our former competitors to interview our former employees. Almost all of the professionals found jobs very quickly, and about half the factory workers landed jobs within a week or two. It took about six more months to sell off our assets and to sell our operations in Singapore and Bangkok.

WHO INVENTS

(A Sapphic Poem[3])

Riemann teased, "We do not invent anything out of
Thin air. Concepts, laws and ideas existed."
Before the void, yea, alas, before humans.
Be thou humble!

Nature's unified theory defeats our best thinkers,
We chip and chip for answers and get epsilons,
Someday all will come together exposing all
Nature's secrets.

Sometimes abstract ideas produce nuggets:
Fibonacci concocted a divergent
Sequence with a limiting ratio of tau
With no purpose,

Fifteen hundred years before,
the Greeks found *tau*.
In the Golden Mean of the perfect rectangle,
But the chambered nautilus preceded them both.
Genius nature!

Riemann appears to be right selectively.
It works far too randomly for assurance,
Man does invent contrary to the belief
Held by Riemann.

CHAPTER IX

Health

A LAMINECTOMY

While walking down the ramp from the ice-skating warming house, I slipped. My legs flew up and I dropped onto a two by four post that stood about six inches out of the ice. I landed with that post hitting me squarely at the small of my back. I walked home across the street and went to bed. I wondered how I got there since my legs no longer moved.

My back hurt, but I had a more urgent problem. I had to go to the bathroom. The pressure built up and we had no bedpan. In desperation we called for an ambulance to get me to a hospital where they supposedly had such conveniences.

At Mount Sinai Hospital in Minneapolis, orderlies put me on a gurney and wheeled me to the receptionist. I asked for a bedpan but the receptionist found it more urgent to ask a million questions about my insurance and health history. I yelled, "Bring me a bedpan."

When I reached the threshold of an explosion, she still ignored my plight. She droned on with, "When did you have small pox?"

To her stupid question, I answered, "If you don't produce an orderly with a bedpan in one second, I'm going to crap right into your gurney."

Two orderlies appeared instantly, each with a bedpan. After filling up one of those receptacles, I noticed that I had a backache, but became civil and coherent.

Her last question was an unexpected one, "What kind of meals do you want?" I chose strictly kosher because I thought I'd get wonderful delicatessen food.

Dr. Karp, my orthopedic surgeon, looked at my X-rays and said, "You have a herniated disc. I will do a laminectomy on L-5 tomorrow morning at eight." He thumbed through the book I brought along, *Patterns of Plausible Inference* by George Polya.

"My son wants to be a mathematician," he said. "I'd like you to tell him about the life of a mathematician." I did so a few days later. This led to a brilliant exchange of professional fees; Dr. Karp charged me only $125 for his surgical services.

I shared a room with Dan, a brakeman for the Great Northern Railroad, who had the same back problem that I did. With a successful operation behind him, he walked around. He had two defects: he smoked and told great jokes I had never heard before.

I thought being in the hospital would give me an opportunity to quit smoking. Far from quitting, we chain-smoked into the night, ruining my resolve. My back hurt so much the slightest motion caused tremors. Even so, his funny jokes sent me into whoops of uncontrollable laughter, followed immediately by convulsions from the pain. I asked Dan to save the jokes until after my operation.

The next day, the doctor performed a "textbook" surgery on my back. The fifth disc had exploded and the fiber poked into the spinal cord. He trimmed the fibers and left the hollow disc in place.

While in the recovery room I thought only about how wonderful it would be, kicking the smoking habit. Such pleasant thoughts disappeared as the effects of the numbing drugs wore off. The cure hurt ten times as much as the injury.

When the nurse wheeled me back to the room, Dan tried to ease my pain by putting a lighted cigarette in my mouth. It tasted so good, I decided to quit some other time.

To make the pain tolerable, the doctor prescribed a wonderful drug called Demarol. One pill converted me from a writhing maniac to a serenely happy person. Now, I listened to Dan's jokes and enjoyed every one to the fullest without the slightest pain in the back. In just one day, I became hooked on those "happy pills." Dr. Karp noticed I enjoyed them too much and cut me back to three a day. Too bad! I hurt most of the time excepting for those three glorious half-hours of euphoria.

The nurse announced, "We are having a sponge bath today." With a smirk, she handed me a soaped washcloth and said, "That's for washing your jewels."

When I asked for a urinal, she said, "Today, we are going to the bathroom to tinkle." Sitting up hurt so much, I decided that henceforth, I'd be a quadruped. With two sturdy nurses supporting me, we went to tinkle.

In the meantime, not one bit of the so-called kosher food arrived. It was mostly stuff like macaroni with brown juice on it. I endured the miserable food without complaining. On the last day, the Kosher Cook popped into my room and said, "I've heard about Japanese Jews but never met one. I had to see you before you checked out." I thanked her. Unfortunately, I didn't have a good punch line. That gem was invented about twenty years later. Howard Appleman told me the joke which went as follows: Dr. Abraham Schwartz, a rabbinical scholar, living in New York heard about a colony of Chinese Jews who lived in isolation for generations in a village in China. This scholar went to that village where the elders, all Chinese, greeted him cordially in Hebrew. The New Yorker asked, "Are you really Jewish." They nodded solemnly and with a puzzled look asked, "But are you Jewish? You don't look Jewish."

When I returned to work a couple of weeks later, my co-workers surrounded me and asked about the operation. I mentioned that in spite of all that pain and poor kosher food, I had not lost an ounce of weight. When they gave me an enema, I lost five pounds instantly. One of my friends observed, "That only proves what I always thought you were full of."

MY EYES

Because I was an executive of a large corporation, I was getting better health care than most people in the general population. Yearly physicals were required, as were regular trips to the dentist and the eye doctor.

Unfortunately for me, I chose an aging ophthalmologist who took care of my eyes for many years.

When he died, I went to his younger partner for an exam. He examined my eyes and shouted, "You have an advanced stage of low tension glaucoma. Why weren't you treated for this condition?"

I sputtered, "Your deceased partner examined me for years and never mentioned the word glaucoma. He must not have tested for it."

"Damn!" he said after reviewing my chart. "He tested only your pressure. That won't detect your kind of glaucoma. Yours is rare. Eighteen millimeters is normal for most people, but that's disastrous for you! We have to keep your pressure under twelve. Ten would be better. I gather my former associate never checked your peripheral vision."

The evil thought that flashed through my head was, if he were going to die anyhow, why hadn't he died early enough that my vision could have been saved.

I've thought a lot about this. I was really angry at that old man for missing the diagnosis, because, of all the things I don't want to lose, sight is right at the top of the scale. Of the five senses, I'd be willing to give up the auditory sense first and vision last. Unfortunately, we are not given such choices.

In studying about my disease, I've learned that about two percent of Americans have it. Most are older people. It is a most insidious malady, for there is no pain, and it happens so gradually that you don't notice it until it is too late. Even more disturbing, ophthalmologists have no idea what causes it.

Glaucoma is an abnormal condition of the eye caused by excessive pressure in the eye itself. For most people, as the young doctor told me, that pressure is about eighteen millimeters of Mercury, or about .35 pounds per square inch. Pressure excesses do great damage to the nerves of the retina surrounding the optic nerve. Excessive pressure causes the optic nerve to invert, which in turn kills the nerves of the retina. As the nerves around the optic blind spot are destroyed, you lose peripheral vision all the way around. Put another way, your cone of vision becomes narrow. A person with normal vision, when looking straight ahead, should be able to see his hands stretched out from his side. The cone is 180 degrees. When this shrinks to fifteen degrees, you are blind.

The diminution of the cone of vision also affects the up and down vision. As I walk around the house, I no longer see open cupboard doors or obstacles on the floor. I have stepped off of loading docks into free space because I didn't see the edge. In fact, that's pretty exciting.

The good news is, they do know how to diagnose and treat

glaucoma. There is no cure, and the treatments are mostly directed at retarding the degradation.

I've been controlling my pressure with eye drops and a series of laser and open-eye surgeries. The most recent one involved cutting a trench one millimeter wide and about four millimeters long on the upper part of the eyeball. This procedure enabled the fluid to seep through the membrane that covered the opening.

It wasn't a fun operation, and for a couple of weeks I had three stitches in each eye. But I did enjoy seeing three of everything. I even got Louise out on the tennis court because I wanted to find out if I could hit the middle ball.

And then my eyelids started to sag. They remained half-closed all day and it looked as if I were asleep. To compensate for this, I used to tilt my head back, since this was easier than opening my eyes wide. This, unfortunately, gave me a snooty look since I really was looking down my nose. Evidently, the muscles that raised and lowered my lids had frayed and partially detached. My ophthalmologist, who was already treating me for glaucoma, suggested that I consider a lid operation to open my eyes. With this operation, I'd see twice as well. He sent me to Dr. Anderson, a specialist in St. Paul who did nothing but eyelids.

Dr. Anderson explained that he performs this operation almost daily, and that the success rate is very high. He would detach the lid muscles and reattach them so that, in a relaxed position, my eyes would open fully. He would also do cosmetic surgery by removing a couple of millimeters of eye fold skin.

That sounded like a reasonable explanation.

"Have you done this procedure with Asian eyes?" I asked.

"No, I've never done one. But I have a good friend in Los Angeles, Dr. Tanaka, who is an expert on Asian eyes. I'll consult with him, and I'll also read the literature on the subject. I should be ready in about a week."

"I suggest you do become an expert. I don't want to change the racial features of my eyes. I want them to remain almond-shaped and squinty just like they were when I had taut eye muscles."

"I assure you, this will be a successful procedure," he said, pulling out a few before and after pictures of his patients. I had to admit the "after" pictures looked better.

"Okay," I said. "Let's go." I signed all the papers to release him from the consequences of a mistake and we made a date.

On the appointed day, I arrived at the Group Health Hospital in St. Paul. After donning the traditional hospital gown, I got into bed and was wheeled into the operating room. Dr. Anderson introduced me to the other surgeon and the two nurses who would be assisting.

The team strapped me down from head to foot so that I couldn't move. Then they taped my head to the operating table. I could move only my eyes and the lids. Dr. Anderson explained that he would inject Novocain around the orbits of both eyes. The anesthesiologist would not put me under because he would need my cooperation testing the eyelids before he closed the incision.

Then they began. I felt nothing. The four of them were chatting as though doing something mindless like shelling peas.

"I had my dog fixed yesterday. He's so cute. He carries around the rubber doll I gave him all day long."

"My cat had kittens. They are all different colors. Do you want one?"

"Hand me a number four knife."

"Oh darn, I forgot to order them. How would a number two do? Oh, here's a used number three. How about that one? I've cleaned it."

"Give me the number two."

"Does anyone want a kitten?"

Through frantic eyes I tried to order them to pay attention to my eyelids. Forget your damned dogs and cats, I commanded. Don't distract the surgeon.

But they went right on with their conversation.

Finally, Dr. Anderson said, "I've connected the muscles temporarily, Carl. I want you to open your eyes as wide as you can."

I complied.

"Good. Now open them to the relaxed position."

Again I moved the lids.

"I see I have to shorten the left one half a millimeter."

"My niece is taking the brown kitten. It's so nice for a young child to have a pet to play with."

And so they continued through the rest of the surgery. Their chitchat about animals and good movies sank my confidence to zero. I figured out that they were finished when they started talking about the next patient in the assembly line.

After they moved me into the recovery room, I remained motionless. The doctor came around to tell me that everything had gone well and that I could go home. "I'll remove the bandages in two days when you come in for your post-op checkup."

I didn't peek, but I did wonder what I looked like. When the surgeon removed the bandages, I looked in the mirror and wasn't thrilled to see that I looked like a raccoon with blood shot eyes.

"You screwed up," I told him. "These are occidental eyes. Are you sure Dr. Tanaka does it like this?"

But there was no turning back. These would be my eyelids for the rest of my life. It was not what I wanted, but I was now able to see twice as well through eyes that opened fully.

A decade later, I learned that it was impossible to do the operation without forming a fold like the eyelid of non-Asians. It took that long to realize that Dr. Anderson and his chatty staff had done okay.

QUITTING SMOKING

I was at the end of a business trip, waiting to board a plane at the Denver International Airport. I took that last drag from a cigarette and shoved it into the sand of the cylindrical ashtray. When I glanced ahead, I saw an angry woman stomping in my direction. She shoved her snout to within inches of my face and bellowed, "You polluting pig."

This enraged person turned to the ashtray where my discarded butt was still emitting a tiny curl of smoke. She snuffed it out with a flourish, punctuating this deed with a menacing glare while waggling her finger at me. Then she clacked away on her high-heeled shoes. In her wake, she left a trail of on-lookers who stared alternately at the polluter and the savior of our clean air.

After collecting my composure, I decided that, if my habit caused other people that much pain, I'd quit smoking now. *Finis.* Cold turkey.

The time was 2 P.M., and the date was September 30, 1976. I tossed my third pack of the day of king-sized Chesterfields into the trash can and never smoked again.

Back home, I washed the ashtrays in my cars and removed the cigarette lighters. I threw away all the ashtrays both at home and at my office. I bought several signs that said, "NO SMOKING," "NO FUMAR," "THANKS FOR NOT SMOKING," and, my favorite, "DON'T EVEN THINK ABOUT SMOKING." I put these signs everywhere. During the past twenty-four years, no one has smoked in my office, in my car or in my home.

One New Year's Day, my neighbor, Bob Metcalf, came over to watch the Rose Bowl game. When his system got low on nicotine, he remembered my stern rules about smoking; he put on his storm coat and went outside. That poor guy watched the game through our window in -15° F. weather. But I couldn't relax my rules. I loved smoking and I knew I could get hooked in an instant if someone lit up around me.

The most addicted person I ever knew was Jesus, a migratory farm laborer I met while hoeing sugar beets in Idaho. When Jesus took a deep drag, he held the smoke in his lungs for several seconds before exhaling. He let out the smoke only a few inches from his mouth. Then he captured that cloud and sent it back to his lungs for a second pass. He rocked the smoke back and forth a few times so that, when he finally exhaled fully, nothing but pure air came out.

Jesus smoked his cigarettes until his fingers burned. His two cigarette-holding fingers had hardened to tough brown calluses. At the next stage, he pierced the butt with a toothpick for a few more inhalations. When the stub became too short for the tooth pick trick, he held the tiny butt between his yellowed teeth until only ashes remained. This man did not pollute the atmosphere, because he absorbed every trace of nicotine and tars into his lungs and other vital parts. His only pollutant was the tiny speck of an ash he spit out at the end of his smoking orgy. In the meantime he enjoyed it so much that he stood still, bug-eyed and transfixed.

My addiction started when I was stationed at Ft. Bragg. I tried many devices for unshackling myself from this prison, but nothing worked. Once, while walking down Hennepin Avenue in Minneapolis, I tossed a "ciggie" on Fifth Avenue and declared, "That's my last one, forever."

A block later, a stranger stopped me and asked, "Pardon me,

but do you have a light?"

I stood tall, with an evangelical facade, and said, "I'm sorry, but I don't smoke."

That resolve had a short life. So did the others that followed for years. My most successful attempt lasted one hundred and fifty-four days. Then, during a tense moment, when a disaster struck at work, someone handed me a lighted cigarette. It happened so automatically that I didn't even notice I was smoking.

After about twenty-five years of smoking an ever-increasing number of cigarettes per day, the doctor who gave me my annual physical said, "Your vital capacity is now low enough that, if one lobe of your lung collapsed, you'd die." Though frightening, that still didn't slow me down. It took the outraged insult from a stranger to persuade me.

Ten years after quitting, my vital capacity rose 10 percent. And today, one lung could fail, but I'd still live.

A VIEW FROM THE END OF THE DRILL

Port Townsend, Washington

My father had the teeth of a *Tyrannosaurus rex*. When he ate a chicken, he crunched its back, neck and the wings and left only the thighbones. He devoured spare ribs the same way. He abused his teeth by opening beer and pop bottles with them. I never saw him brushing his teeth because he didn't own a toothbrush. Sometimes he used a toothpick. Yet he had all thirty-two teeth and no cavities when he died at fifty-four. He never had a toothache and never went to a dentist. What great teeth genes to inherit!

My mother, on the other hand, had the world's worst teeth with super short roots. At thirty-five, she had full dentures. By the luck of the draw, I inherited her hopeless teeth. Whenever I went to a new dentist, he'd look at my X-rays, and immediately call in his partner, saying, "Hey, Joe, come look at the short roots on this guy's teeth."

I married a person with saber-toothed tiger teeth. Louise's had thick enamel and super-long roots. When she went to a new dentist, he would call his partner and say, "Hey, Joe, look at the X-rays of these long roots."

How fortunate my children are! They have *Tyrannosaurus rex* or saber-toothed tiger teeth.

My problems started when I was seventeen. I was playing catch with Junior McCabe, and we were using a croquet ball. When that got boring, we started tossing two of the balls, trying to keep one of them in the air at all times. When I missed a ball and bent over to pick it up, the next ball hit me in the mouth. It knocked out the tooth the dentists call number ten.

For ten dollars, I had a bridge put in. That was a lot of money in 1939, and I tried to be more careful about my teeth after that. That bridge lasted for thirty years. Then a supporting tooth of the bridge gave way. I was then missing two teeth instead of one. A dentist in Minneapolis fitted me with a bridge by shaping one more adjoining tooth to serve as an anchor. But over the next several years, those support teeth kept failing in succession, like falling dominoes. Finally, my anchor teeth were so far apart that my bridge looked like a wobbly fence supported only by distant corner posts.

I was, by then, living in Port Townsend and happily retired. My dentist gave me three options: be fitted with a permanent or removable bridge, pull out all remaining upper teeth and get dentures or implants.

I chose the latter option. My dentist estimated my total tab at about $18,000. This estimate was about right if I hadn't had surgery for the sinus lift that I will describe later. So why would an advanced senior citizen like me get teeth that would outlast me by three centuries when I didn't even buy the economy size box of cereal in case I wouldn't use it all up?

It was because I didn't want to get an ever lengthening and swaying bridge that was ready to crash every six months. Besides, who wants to be a toothless, slobbering old man? I wanted a "Pepsodent" smile.

At the appointed date, the periodontist asked, "Do you have any questions?"

"How many teeth?"

"Three," he replied. "Maybe four if the bone of number seven is wide enough. I'll have to cut it open to find out."

"Let's do it."

"Are you allergic to anything?"

"Yes. Novocain. I overreact to it. My eye surgeon suggested asking for a half dose."

Dr. Osterberg, the oral surgeon, had two assistants. One handled the sprayer and the suction, the other supplied instruments and other dental aids. Lying flat on my back, I couldn't see anything they were doing, I could only surmise. Dr. Osterberg showed me the template he would use for aligning the screw holes to my upper jawbone. "I could do this by eye, but I want to be more accurate, because your bone is narrow," he said.

How considerate!

After the Novocain took effect, he began to cut. "The gum must be fibrous," I thought because the cutting made the same sound you get from cutting a turkey's gizzard across the grain.

"Give me the drill with the long shank," he said.

I stifled a gasp. Using the template, he began to drill. I visualized a drill bit about an eighth of an inch in diameter. And, since he didn't have a straight shot, I figured the drill motor might have been a right-angled Black-and-Decker. Once he had the holes started, he removed the template and began drilling in earnest.

Though there aren't supposed to be very many nerves in the bone, he managed to hit every one of them—some several times. I writhed in agony.

He gave me more shots of Novocain and continued drilling. Though in some situations I am overly sensitive to the numbing drug, the pain at that moment was so intense I could have handled a dose large enough to make a kitten out of a musk-ox.

As he worked, Dr. Osterberg maintained a steady monologue, most of which was incomprehensible to me, "Mumble . . . two more millimeters . . . mumble . . ."

His assistants seemed to understand him, because they responded by handing him instruments or by doing something like washing away the blood, which had to be there. I thought maybe I wasn't understanding him because my brain was paralyzed from the Novocain. But I found out later that he had been talking to himself in Swedish.

As I bolted almost upright when he hit a nerve, he said, "Sorry, Carl."

I thought he was being insincere, since he went right on hurting me. In retrospect, there probably is no comment he could have made that would have lessened the pain.

When he finally completed the drilling of his four holes, he put in the screws with a motorized right-angle screwdriver. The procedures were beginning to look like carpentry. The titanium screws were fifteen millimeters long. With his machine, he sank in all but the final two millimeters. Then we reached the painful part. He hand-screwed those final millimeters with a little wrench.

My bone creaked and moaned in protest at this invasion. My head turned from the torque. Between onslaughts, I tried to have lovely thoughts about beautiful women. Instead, pained questions dominated my thoughts: "Was there any chance the bone would split like wood when screwed with such force? Could the screws overshoot and come out somewhere on the face?"

I counted twelve half-turns to advance the screw two millimeters. This worked out to three full turns per millimeter. A rapid calculation suggested about seventy-five threads per inch. That would be as fine as the threads of the screws in the hinges of eyeglass frames.

He continued to hand-screw.

When I gave him a wild-eyed look, he gave that spot a rest and moved on to the next screw.

That short rest seemed to relieve the pain. But the screw tightening was interminable.

At long last he finished. Two and a half hours had gone by. He sewed the gum together and buried the heads of the screws. He would do no more surgery for six months in order to allow the bone to relax from its intense compression and allow it to bond firmly to the screws. He prescribed penicillin and pain killers. His assistant gave me a bill for $3,970, which included a 10 percent discount for cash.

I returned a week later to have the sutures removed. While I was there, I asked the dental technician to show me a titanium screw. On examination, I found that I was off by a factor of two in my estimates. The sizes of drills and screws must go up in direct proportion to the level of pain.

My imagination went wild. The drill could not have been

more than 1/16th of an inch in diameter. The titanium screw looked like a small self-tapping sheet metal screw with a hex head except that it probably costs a thousand times as much. Why titanium, I wondered? Perhaps there's something special in the metal. In fact, titanium is a refractory metal with a coefficient of thermal expansion that matches the jawbone.

Six months later, the periodontist cut my gum to install screws called healing caps. When the gum had healed around those caps, Dr. Griffith, my dentist, had the crown made for the four front upper teeth, and then screwed the crown into the titanium screws with the inside threads. Dr. Griffith is a dedicated woman who often thinks about my teeth at 10:30 P.M. and calls to tell me her latest plan. Once she advised, "Since the crowns are screwed in, the screws might have to be tightened once in a while."

She was right. Three years later, a screw loosened. So I called Dr. Osterberg's office. The receptionist asked why I needed an appointment, and then announced for all to hear, "Your patient, Nomura, has a screw loose in his head."

That brought an almost instantaneous response from the periodontist and, within a few hours, he tightened the loose screw.

Though I could sense the movement of the crown, the periodontist could not detect a motion. Three turns of one screw did the job. Coincidentally, the same procedure would adjust the carburetor on my '74 VW Super Beetle.

There were more teeth to be done at the back of my jaw, but they couldn't proceed. With teeth going in and out, my bite had gone to ruin. My jaws ached from traveling beyond where they should have because there was no normal biting pattern. This was urgent. My dentist said we needed to get a measurement of where my bite should be. To accomplish this, she took me to the University of Washington where a senior dentistry professor made extensive measurements to locate that invisible line that would become my bite. I still needed three upper right molars. Unfortunately, the jawbone had become too thin for implantation from the lack of use and because of a sinus cavity above the back jawbone. This required surgery called the "sinus lift." To thicken the jaw, a peri-odontist and a surgeon from the University of Washington School of Dentistry, sawed a bone out of my pelvis. It measured about 1 by ¾ by 2 ½ inches. They then shaped that bone to fit snugly against the jawbone from inside the sinus cavity. That bone implant was pulled tightly against the jawbone by loops of stainless steel wire twisted at the ends and tightened as you would a bale of hay. An X-ray showed the wires with the twisted ends bent over and lying against the bone under the gum.

The hip surgery left my leg black and blue for a long time. This hurt a great deal more than the dentistry. A couple of years later, an X-ray showed that the hole in the hip had filled with regenerated bone, leaving only a dimple on each side.

Six months later, the pelvis bone implant bonded securely to give me a jawbone as stout as a Neanderthal's. The periodontist took out the twisted wires and screwed in more titanium screws as described earlier. Six months later, I finally got my three back teeth. The whole procedure, involving two dentists, two periodontists, an orthopedic surgeon and an anesthesiologist, took two and a half years because I got my teeth in two waves, the front ones first, the back ones later. The total tab from beginning to end was $28,000, but a large part of that was the hip surgery.

The outcome of all this activity with my real and synthetic teeth was that I had a perfect bite and teeth that looked better and were stronger than the original ones. With my new set of *Tyranno-saurus rex* teeth, I crunch chicken necks and spare ribs just like my father did. I also abandoned the idea I read in a "Dear Abby" column many years ago: one old codger danced the Flamenco using his dentures as castanets!

Would I do it again? Yes, without the slightest hesitation. The results are so superior to any other alternative. Now I am beautiful and I flash my smile at every opportunity. Those teeth will be good until the year 2296. So, for a good return on my investment, I must stay healthy and live a long time.

CHAPTER X

Retirement

PREPARATION

Minneapolis, Minnesota

To retire does not mean retreating to a rocking chair to watch a sequoia inch its way skyward. It means not going to work. You can no longer think TGIF (Thank God it's Friday), because you don't care whether it's Friday or any other day of the week. Far from going into a state of inactivity, it is the opposite.

Retired people I know utter the same sentence as though they had invented it: "I'm so busy now, I don't know how I found the time to work."

It's a great phase of life so long as you keep all the parts from wearing out too fast.

Before retiring, we took a company seminar with the seductive title, "Successful Retirement." We sat through many weeks of presentations on budgets, Social Security, and health insurance. The seminar director then sent us into the world with her quintessential pearls of success. She said, "Don't sell your house, don't move away, don't buy a house, don't marry and don't divorce."

We sold our house in Minneapolis, moved away and bought a house. I suppose we could have divorced and married just to be defiant. We didn't because we ran out of time for frivolous activities. After violating three-fifths of the "don'ts," we ventured forth to see what awaited us.

Instead of the typical gold watch, friends and colleagues passed the hat and raised enough to buy me a sixteen-foot Crestliner bass fishing boat with a trailer. Bob Grangoth, the instigator, must have gone around the company and collected funds by putting a forty-five to their heads.

In addition, the CEO, Ed Spencer, presented me with a sterling silver plate for thirty-three years of service. He said, "Carl has made a greater contribution to Honeywell than any other executive."

Before we left, Louise staged a garage sale and sold about half of our carefully acquired possessions by reclassifying them as junk. Some good stuff was sold by accident, such as my $150 ski suit that went for five bucks. The great mystery was why the clunky baggage-hauling cart used by porters at railroad stations remained a treasure and was moved 1,800 miles across the country. Louise's slogan—"Everything must go"—became a reality when she sold the house and *my* car at this three-day garage sale.

We waved goodbye to the friends we made during our forty-three year stay in Minnesota. We left behind the mosquitoes. We abandoned the forty-below weather and a very high state income tax.

We wanted adventures. Don Quixote found his by dropping his reins and prodding Rosinante. We took no such chance. We headed straight west. Unlike lemmings, we did not fling ourselves into the sea. Instead, we stopped a quarter of a mile short of Elliott

Bay in the State of Washington and rented an apartment to explore the state and to find a house. After searching for six months, we got tired of looking and bought a condo on Queen Anne Hill in Seattle.

PORT TOWNSEND

When the temperature sank to a record low of eight degrees, I realized we hadn't escaped from Siberia. We rushed to Florida for warmth and to play tennis. Teri called us in Naples to tell us, "We found the perfect house for you in Port Townsend. But to get it you have to decide now. You don't have time to think about it. I also need $800 of earnest money and I don't have that much."

One of the things that happen when you retire is that kids you used to boss around now begin calling the shots. So, like a good retired father, I trusted the kid and her judgment and said, "Give them a check and ask them to hold it. I'll make it good when I get back in ten days."

The "perfect house" turned out to be a run-down dump appraised at an inflated value of $18,000. But it sat on seven acres with a panoramic view of Port Townsend and the municipal golf course. Many bucks and one year later, we moved in. We put away the tools and declared the renovation done when we reached the "creeping elegance" stage.

The greatest attraction of this town has always been the people. The uniqueness is that most live here because of the quality of life not attainable elsewhere. It is a community of well-educated and talented people with no pretension. They are incredibly easy to meet.

Those in town who are bridge, poker and tennis players share my interests. But so do the writers, discussion group members, computer buffs, mushroom enthusiasts, gardeners, woodworkers, Great Books discussion people, and members of the church. Throw in exercisers, line and contra dancers, politicians, board members, school task forces, fund-raisers, fishing buddies, travelers, gourmet cooks, and partiers, and at this point, I'm in touch with most of the people in town. What is a person to do with this vast cornucopia of goodies? Do them all, of course.

For a bridge nut like me, this is heaven. I play duplicate bridge for master points in Sequim, Chimacum and Port Townsend. If I wanted to become a better player quickly, I could take lessons from experts who live nearby.

The Port Townsend Tennis Club organizes a number of events among its members as well as with players from Oak Harbor. We also go to Bainbridge to play on indoor courts during the winter.

The *Tuesday Morning Breakfast Club* is a discussion group of twenty-three people who meet to exchange ideas on a wide range of subjects. We also learn from presentations made by both the members and invited speakers. This group has replaced my work friends.

My special joy is meeting with a group of writers who critique each other's work. They are accomplished writers so that, when they read, I become engrossed in what they are saying. I rarely find flaws. They are my mentors, since I'm the only one still learning to write. With eagle eyes, they zero-in on the key wrong in my work.

In my forays into town, I go to the bank, buy a maple walnut cone at Elevated Ice Cream, and stop to say hello to Lainie at the Franklin House Gallery. The next stop is Bread and Roses where I get a small loaf of French bread. It is so delicious that I eat half of it on the way home. On those nights when I seem to be a quart low on hot and sour soup, I go to the Shanghai Restaurant to refuel.

The most time-consuming activity is my gardening. I enriched the soil with compost and cow manure to make it super-rich. What a joy to have a whole meal of nothing but home-grown produce! Now I'm practicing the art of growing winter vegetables.

I am making the transition to a serene retired life. I've begun to back off from doing everything within sight. Instead, I concentrate on things important to me, such as learning to write and growing fruits and vegetables. Nevertheless, it is my style to do things the hard way. For example, when practical, I use a scythe instead of a weed-eater. If I hire someone to help me, I choose to do the harder tasks, such as wheelbarrow work. To balance this frenzy of activity, I practice being calm by picking the longest line at the supermarket and following slow cars without becoming catatonic. Finally, I take the time to play with and to listen carefully to what my grandchildren are saying.

There is no better place to go into active retirement than Port Townsend. People in far away places like Myrtle Beach or Mission Viejo exclaim, "I know Port Townsend. What a lovely place to live."

My local friends warn me with, "Shut up. Don't let this secret out." But I really do have the people and everything else I need right here.

THE ADJUSTMENT

In the meantime, I had to make many changes in my life from one in which "everything is important" to "nothing is important." I used to be an expert in several things in my former occupations. Now, I'm a rank amateur in absolutely everything I do. At Honeywell, many people were assigned to do what I needed done.

Now, I do them all as well as the "honey do" tasks.

Louise, on the other hand, picked up her art, gardening, and everything else that interested her and moved them all to her new locale and friends. Her lifestyle didn't have to change that much.

That's when I decided to farm. My first crop was organically grown garlic. This was the brainstorm of my son-in-law, Mike Bowen. He helped me plant, but then rushed off to the Bering Strait to his fishing job. This left me the enormous job of weeding. Louise and Teri braided the garlic and rented a stall in Seattle's Pike Place Market. The total expense was fifty-two dollars and revenue was forty-eight dollars. This led to the policy of giving away all of our produce.

AN AWARD

In May 1988, I received a letter from Dr. Sauer, President of the University of Minnesota, that stated the Committee on Honors of the Board of Regents had recommended that I be awarded the *Distinguished Graduate/Outstanding Achievement Award* at the winter graduation ceremonies. After receiving a letter of acceptance from me, he would arrange for press releases.

I, of course, accepted but I wondered what the award was since I had never heard of it. I was also puzzled by how the Committee found me, and more importantly, what it thought I had achieved. More information on the details of the ceremony arrived. It was scheduled for October 4, 1988 and would be held at the banquet of Science and Technology Day in Minneapolis, Minnesota.

When the chairperson of the Honors Committee called, he told me that the award is university-wide, and that it is the highest and most prestigious award given to a graduate. The recipient is chosen from a field of 300,000 living graduates. My achievements had been under study for three years. And he told me that my file was three inches thick. Evidently, a lot of people had known what was afoot, but none had betrayed the University since the news was a total surprise to me.

At the ceremony, attended by nine hundred people, the Regent read my citation and then gave me the Outstanding Achievement Award—a medal and a pin. Though I had been instructed to say nothing in response, it was clear that the Regent hadn't gotten the word. He asked me to respond.

Being caught flat-footed, I shot from the hip. "I thank the Board of Regents, the President of the University, Dean Infante and everyone else who made this award possible. This is a humbling experience since I don't think I published anything profound, nor did I invent anything of consequence. It seems that I am being recognized for going to work every day and doing what I thought needed doing.

"I have very fond memories of the University of Minnesota. I think about the many kind things the university did for me during the difficult war years. I also think of the many wonderful professors who taught me everything and, in particular, I thank my Ph.D. thesis advisor Dr. William G. Shepherd. He was my teacher, mentor and friend. Thank you for the award."

My son, John, who listened to my talk, thought that I made a very humble statement.

I returned home to Port Townsend and wondered how many rows of garlic I should plant that year. The Dean wrote that he was enjoying the braid of garlic I gave him.

THE SEX LIFE OF THE OCTOPUS

Port Angeles, Washington

Several years ago I signed up for an Elderhostel week that featured creative writing and Plato's Republic. In preparation for that week I packed my word processor and checked in at Peninsula College in Port Angeles, Washington. At the orientation session, strange things began to happen. The first instructor introduced was an expert on the octopus, the next a tree specialist and the third a marine biologist. Where was Phyllis Miletich, the creative writing teacher? I said to her on the last day of her class: "I'll see you in creative writing class." How about the platonic scholar? I came the wrong week! This was "Marine Life in the Olympic Peninsula Week."

When I explained my problem to the Elderhostel Coordinator, he threw an apoplectic fit and sputtered, "First, the week you signed up for happened last week. Six hundred people applied for this highly prized course so names had to be drawn for the chosen few. Now by accident you occupy the coveted slot of a more deserving person." After this blast, I suddenly became interested in biology and chose to study the flora, fauna and marine life of the Olympic Peninsula.

The best part was on the sex life of the octopus. The male's sex organ is at the tip of his third right arm while the female's is a pouch-like thing on her body. When mating time comes around, a male roams around the ocean bottom looking for a female of the same species. When he finds one that appeals to him, the sneaky rascal sits next to her with an innocent look on his face while probing for that pouch. He deposits his sperm and then slinks off to expire. A female octopus certainly doesn't look like she is worth dying for, but the males do it all the time.

Later the female lays her eggs and hangs them on the ceiling of a cave where they incubate in freely flowing water. She guards the eggs with ferocity and stops eating for several months. When they hatch, she dies as the young swim off to be gobbled by predators. This is a watery *Romeo and Juliet* tragedy with the lovers dying and even in the same order.

Once in a while we find a giant octopus. It is a virgin who never found a mate and therefore keeps growing. I thought of an alternative explanation: maybe some are left-handed and use the wrong digit—they need counseling.

This much knowledge in one week was worth the trip.

MIDORI

Port Townsend, Washington

When Teri was thirty-seven years old, she decided she would not have a second child because of the increased risk of fetal defects by older mothers. She was so sure of her decision, she bet her home-town friends, the Amersons, $100. Little did she suspect that nine months later she would give birth to a girl who she named Midori. The name means green in Japanese and it is a name shared by the concert violinist and the Olympic figure skating medalist. She is 1/2 Japanese, 5/64 Scottish, 1/64 Choctaw Indian, 3/16 English and 7/32 Irish. From that rich gene pool, she extracted the best from her ancestors. She wore size eight shoes at nine years of age, which suggests that she will grow tall. Teri, very happily, paid her lost bet for this prize.

Midori's first job was to provide the background for my message on the phone machine. I waited patiently for her to cry. I recorded her squall and recorded, "Heh, heh, let me call you later. I'm busy with an unhappy, wet baby." The responses I got were, "When are you going to change that baby's diaper?" or, "That baby needs a dry diaper." This message was such a distraction to callers, many forgot to leave any message.

When I was baby-sitting eighteen-month-old Midori, she often got into mischief such as rolling out the toilet paper while I worked on a story in the next room. Then one day I heard a thump and a splash. I knew in an instant what had happened. I rushed to the bathroom. I threw aside the Lucite cover of my Japanese soaking tub. It was twenty-seven inches deep. There I found her submerged and struggling under a foot of water. I snatched her out and held her upside down as she sputtered out water and cried out. That life saving experience has formed a special bond between the child and me.

Being a most active child, she checked out everything in my house. She unscrambled my computer, pasted postage stamps on the wall and made crayon scribbles everywhere; her threes were written backward. On one of her excursions, she got into my medicine cabinet and ate some of my strong relaxant pills called Flexeril. It's a thin pill only 3/16 inches in diameter and yet powerful enough to cure my back pain. When I found the pill bottle on the floor, I counted the pills remaining in the bottle and decided she took six. We found six of the remains of the pills she spit out after she dissolved the sweet coating. If she had taken them internally the consequence would have been most severe since that dosage was lethal enough to make a purring kitten out of a raging Texas longhorn bull.

Once the two girls and an older boy were on their way to Seattle with Teri. The boy bragged, "I've been to California and to

Montana." Sumiko said, "I've been to Minnesota, Rome, Florence, Los Angeles and Portland." Not to be outdone, Midori quipped, "I've been to roller skating."

"Mido" kept disappearing at the Seattle Center, which was filled with all kinds of play equipment and furry animals that the kids could touch. In desperation, Teri took the strap off her purse and hooked it on Midori. Finding herself on a leash, Mido dropped to all fours on the floor, and to the delight of the passersby, she said, "Woof, woof."

When she was four, I invited Mido and her sister to color Easter eggs. Lucille Watson loved this activity but had no kids around to help her color her eggs so I invited her to join us. In minutes she appeared with eighteen hard boiled eggs ready for decorating. While we worked on the eggs Lucille made small talk with Midori: "Wouldn't you like to have a little brother?" She answered, "Yes I would but that is not possible."

"Why?"

"Because my mother had her tubes tied."

Poor Lucille expired on the spot from shock.

When the two family cats Sally and Loopo had kittens, there was much discussion about how all that happened. They also figured that the tomcat down the street was the father because many of the kittens had tiger stripes. Thus, at the age of six, Midori drew some conclusions about the differences between men and women. Next day, when she talked to the neighbor, she said, "Men are unlucky."

"Why?"

"Because men don't have tits."

"What do you mean men don't have tits?" He pulled up his T-shirt and said, "See I've got them." Midori scoffed at his tiny protuberances and declared, "When I grow up, I'm going to have big ones." A well endowed friend hearing this story, quipped, "If she takes after her mother, she's in for a disappointment."

Midori collects all kinds of critters such as newts, frogs, bugs, and snakes. Insects are her special passion so for her birthday, she asked for a bug cage. Once when she found one more bug than she could hold in her hands, she popped it in her mouth for safe-keeping until she found a jar.

Now at age nine, she is emerging a beauty with a happy and most captivating personality. She went to her father's reunion in Minnesota. There everyone had to make nametags so the rascal wrote, "not telling" on hers and had great fun teasing everyone. They responded by calling her "Blossom."

FOURTEEN HOURS IN NAIROBI

Naibori, Kenya

Lucille and Lars Watson agreed to join Louise and me on a trip to Kenya. The year was 1994 and we were, among other things, go-ing to visit my friend Joe Elliott, who was on a Peace Corp assign-ment. Joe was a retired teacher and was now living in Masii, a primitive village 200 kilometers from Nairobi. Good times lay ahead.

We had just come through customs and met our tour guide from Nissan Safaris.

"I need to change some money," I said, thinking of the tips I would soon be required to pay.

"I'll take you to the bank," our driver agreed. He waved the others to seats in the main hall while escorting me to a nearby branch of the Kenyan Bank.

I hate standing in lines, but in this case I figured I had no choice. I needed Kenyan shillings because I heard that foreign currency is illegal in Kenya.

The line was long and everyone wore the mask of disgust as dust and trash swirled around us. The queue was made up of Europeans, Americans, Far East Asians, Indians and black Africans. The two black men in front of me were as different as two people could be. One, who towered over me at almost seven feet, was 300 pounds of solid muscle. The other was an elderly and delicate gentleman in a white suit, perfectly proportioned but no bigger than an eight-year-old.

People craned their necks to see why each transaction took so long. The man at the head of the line conducted a lengthy and vociferous debate with the clerk in Swahili, but he slunk away empty-handed. As an old lady proffered her money to a clerk, a boisterous man came from nowhere, shoved her aside, and began his transaction. Evidently the clerk had the policy of serving whoever was standing in front of him. Nobody said anything. The line undulated sideways as anger bristled in the air.

Time dragged on. Though February, it is blazing hot in Equatorial Africa. Nevertheless, I was glad to be there. I daydreamed about the animals I would see on safaris in two game reserves— Amboseli in the north, and the Masai Mara in the south.

A second man, who crowded into the head of the line, interrupted my reverie. The giant black man stepped forward, spun the intruder around, grabbed him by his lapels and raised him a foot and a half into the air to his own eye level. He snarled, "If you want to live, go to the end of the line."

He dropped the man on his heels as coins clattered to the concrete. Nobody helped the line crasher, now sprawled in the street.

The tiny gentleman in white, under the protective eyes of his gargantuan friend, squeaked, "Hey, old boy, go to the back."

One hour later, I reached the clerk's cage and turned sideways to prevent anyone from crowding in front of me. The clerk, sallow and not shiny black like the other young men, studied my passport carefully as though it were a hot novel. He took my money and waited with a stone face as I filled out a long form. Then he counted my money several times and passed it and the paperwork through a hole into the counting room. After several minutes, a pile of shillings and my documents came through the hole.

The clerk recalculated the conversion figure three times and then counted the money twice. He counted it again as he gave it to me. The money was dirty and faded from use, but carefully folded into bundles of 1,000 shillings. The worried look on the clerk's face made me wonder what severe penalty he suffered for making any kind of error.

When I joined my traveling companions, Lucille and Lars Watson and my wife, Louise, they took turns blasting me.

"Why did it take so long?"

"Why didn't you go to the bank right there? Those lines dissolved in minutes?"

I stuttered, "But, but, gasp, choke, Jeremiah, our Safari Agent, took me to the other bank."

Feathers unruffled as we loaded our baggage onto the Nissan Safari Van. Life looked a lot better as we gazed at the manicured trees, but the scene changed abruptly when we entered Nairobi with its teeming mass of people. Rock music and auto horns merged with vehicle noises. The buildings were a mixture of super-modern and dilapidated structures.

The Nissan, with its top raised, plowed through a sea of Kenyans clogging Tom Myoba Street. As the driver inched toward the curb to park, vendors dangled their beads and carvings through the window shouting, "Only 200 shillings."

Beggars thrust their maimed or leprous hands through the window and asked for shillings.

I shrank from the explosion of demands.

The porter and guards of the Hotel Prince, shouted them aside while making sure they didn't touch the one without fingers.

The leper hobbled back by hooking his arm over a pole with a "Y" on its top.

We walked through a corridor of more beggars with shocking disfigurements. Nobody had a crutch. They had poles that shone from use. A quadriplegic shouted, "Your American bombs did this to me. Pay me."

The sticky heat added to the discomfort of seeing so much misery and smelling the stench of poverty.

When I stepped into the lobby, my world transformed. It was one with shiny floors, crystal chandeliers, over-stuffed sofas, and elegantly dressed people. This change was just as shocking as entering the beggars' world had been only a moment before. And these two realities were only twenty feet apart.

I thought I had re-entered the twentieth century, but that wasn't true. The pretty receptionist, Michelle, with her beautifully coiffured hair piled high, told me they had no reservations for our party of four. My voucher and acknowledgment of prepayment made no difference. We appealed to Tom, the head clerk, who listened with surliness and then disappeared for twenty minutes while we twiddled our thumbs.

When he returned, he had found our confirmations. Tom must have filed them in a bushel basket. This was a pretty good guess, since the scene was repeated two days later when we tried to check out. That time, it took thirty minutes to find our confirmations and acknowledgment of prepayment.

The only clue that this hotel was in the service business was the cheerful and efficient porter named Daniel. (All the Kenyans we met had Christian first names and unpronounceable last names that started with double consonants such as Mb, Ng or Nk.) We put our things onto the elevator and went up. It stopped twenty inches below our second floor hall. To give it a second try, the porter went to the third floor and then came down. This time, the mismatch was only ten inches, so we climbed out of the hole.

Our room overlooked the street with its beggars, bumper-to-bumper cars and minivans (called *mutatus*) with wailing air horns that announced their arrivals. The *mutatus* were designed for eight passengers, but had been fashioned with seats to shoehorn in twenty or more, thus filling every cubic centimeter of space with bodies. To add to the confusion, several rock music stations competed with one another. This was going to be a sleepless night.

There was no hot water, so we took lukewarm baths. Much refreshed, we ate at the hotel restaurant, which was featuring a Kenyan smorgasbord. Except for some of the fruits, chicken and beef, everything was unfamiliar. The most startling was the white stuff that looked like Cream of Wheat. It turned out to be scrambled eggs made with eggs with colorless yolks. The greens tasted like collards and kale. Tripe was a featured delicacy, perhaps because it was not tough like their beef. Though different, everything tasted good.

Weary from travel the eleven-hour-time change and no sleep for thirty-six hours, I went to bed at 8:00 P.M. and was instantly asleep. Louise, who had taken many catnaps, was not sleepy, so she went to visit the Watsons in the next room. She returned about forty-five minutes later. Something was wrong. She was disturbed because everything seemed to have been moved around the room. Why had I put the passports on the dresser? She couldn't sleep.

Something was wrong.

At 11:45 P.M. the phone rang. It was the security guard who wanted to see me immediately. At the front desk, the guard and several hotel employees were staring at my briefcase. It had been slashed across both diagonals. A guest in a room two doors away from ours had found it in the hall with its contents scattered. My wallet, with credit cards and $300 in travelers' checks, money belt, and an electric shaver were missing. A burglar had entered our unlocked room while I slept and Louise visited next door. The guard couldn't understand how anyone could get to the second floor without going past him at the entrance.

After being interrogated by a detective from Central Police Station for two hours, I returned to my room with the resolve that I would forget the traumas of the past fourteen hours and enjoy Africa. I collapsed on the bed without bothering to take off my clothes and shoes, merely counting my lucky stars that I hadn't awakened while I was being robbed. My throat could have looked like that briefcase.

JIM WESTALL

Jim Westall, a high school special education teacher, used innovative ways of developing new skill for students with disabilities such as Down's Syndrome, schizophrenia, autism, fetal alcohol and drug syndromes. He started a food catering business with the students preparing the food. Later he had them making jump ropes by stringing beads. These sold well so he started a jump rope company outside of the school system that he named *Skookum*, a Native American word meaning "well made." He put all of his savings into the company and later obtained loans by using his house as collateral.

One day he spoke to the *Tuesday Morning Breakfast Club* where I was a member. He described some of his difficulties. I offered solutions a couple times because I used to run a non-profit enterprise with the same kinds of problems. He invited me to his office and proposed, "Why don't you be my mentor and show me how to run it and become the Chairman of the Board of Skookum?"

Since I had retired recently, I wasn't looking for work. In fact, I intended to spend all of my time playing. Nevertheless, I was so impressed with Jim (who laid his life on the line for the benefit of his fellow man) I could not refuse. I croaked, "Yes" as I saw my leisure time being carried away by the wind. But I had encountered a *great* man.

The first order of business was to find out why we were losing money and the best candidates were the cost of the products in relationship to their selling price. We found that the beaded ropes cost $3.50 to make and were sold for $1.75. We had to find a cheaper way of making them and we had to increase the prices. We found a couple of mechanical geniuses, Gil Clayton and Bob Garrison, in town who designed mechanisms for stringing those beads by mechanical means rather than by hand. The simple ones made money, but not enough to pay for the losses incurred by the beaded ropes.

At a brainstorming session, Jim came up with the winning idea: do janitorial work. This led to the generalized concept that we do work that is shunned by people and therefore commanded better pay. We also wanted work that didn't require much skill. Waste management, janitorial work and outdoor toilets were obvious examples. Jim ran with these ideas and developed a profitable business enterprise. The profits from these businesses now support others such as the jump rope company which now must compete with ropes made in China.

Skookum kept improving its managerial skills so that on May 22, 2002, it won the award for being the best-managed company in the nation from among 700 companies that are like Skookum. It is called the *Performance Excellence in Government Contract Award.* In his acceptance speech for the award, Jim thanked me for the fourteen years that I served as his mentor on how to run the business.

From when I joined Skookum, it has grown by fifteen-fold. It generates a good profit much of which Jim plows into several communities as a community service.

YES AND NO IN JAPAN

Tokyo, Japan

In 1992, Louise and I attended an Elderhostel in Japan. I studied Japanese for several months, and Louise brushed up on hers. We planned to visit relatives and friends, thinking our language skills would get us through the tough spots.

Travelers beware! Though equipped with your brand new *Berlitz*, you may be surprised that what you heard might not mean what was meant. Misunderstandings occur even among us in our mother tongue. For instance, have you ever had a guest who said, "But I didn't know we were invited for dinner. We ate before we came."

This has happened to us several times. Now we repeat, "You understand you are invited to have dinner at 6:00 P.M. at our house on Wednesday, May 20?"

If you want to be certain, the trick is to get them to repeat that last sentence and to write it in blood.

At the workplace, I've often said, "But that is not what I said."

Too bad! What the listener understood is what I communicated, no matter what I thought I'd said.

These miscommunications multiply in foreign countries. We experienced disasters several times during our visit to Japan. First, no one understood my "Dick and Jane" version of Japanese. They actually understood my English better. The profound differences in the cultures served as an additional barrier to comprehension.

The most perplexing source of error lies in the meanings of "Yes" and "No." President Richard Nixon returned from Japan with the triumphant message, "They said 'Yes'." But the Prime Minister had actually said, "We will think about it." Translation: A definite No!

Mr. Nixon's misinterpretation caused turmoil in Japan. It is now known as the "Nixon *Shokku* (shock)." Had he known more about the culture, Mr. Nixon would have noticed that no one ever said "No" to any of his questions. Their "Yes" sometimes meant they had understood what was said, and *not* that they agreed.

How does one distinguish the real "yes" from the, "I heard you" kind of yes? One has to learn the cultural meanings: In Japan, a subordinate never says "no" to a superior, since "no" would challenge the superior's knowledge. Thus, an emissary to the Prime Minister who answered some of Nixon's questions never said "no" to the superior he was speaking with, the President of the United States. Can you imagine the garbled messages President Nixon stored in his head during these negotiations?

Dr. Carl Becker, Professor of Philosophy at Tsukuba University in Tokyo gave a wonderful lecture on this problem at our

Elderhostel. He declared:

> " . . . In the Western culture, we have a love affair with symbolic logic. For example, for the statement "A," "not A" means the exact opposite. The Japanese consider these things an interesting but useless abstraction. Their no does not always mean 'not A.' They more often mean 'it is different from A.' If they insist that it is still different from the 'revised A,' then the discussion has gone far-a-field from the original statement . . .
>
> "How do the Japanese ever converge on what was meant by asserting 'it's different' without giving clues on how it is 'different?' The miracle is that they do. I suspect it is done with considerable redundancy in their speech. One persuasive example is that the translation of 'must' requires ten words if you really mean it.
>
> "The Japanese hate saying no. Instead, they might say, 'That is a difficult question.' Though you wait, there are no more answers. The lack of elaboration suggests that it means, 'I don't want to answer that question.'
>
> "An exaggerated sucking in of breath signals another sure bet no. I once served as an interpreter at a negotiation between officials of an American company and a Japanese one. We listened to many long exhortations on how difficult the question was, punctuated by scratching of the head and sucking in of the breath. So, like the translator in

comic scenes in the movies, I compressed the answer to, 'He said no'."

BEGGARS AND VENDORS IN MEXICO

Oaxaca, Mexico

We again ran into beggars when Louise and I visited Oaxaca, Mexico with my hero, Jim Westall. We combed the *mercado* (market) in the mornings and drank coffee in the afternoons at an outdoor café where vendors and beggars accosted us. One of them was a twelve-year-old vendor who stopped to give us a hard-sell two or three times a day. She had very coarse black hair that looked like she'd never combed it. And you could see a clear demarcation between the washed part of the face and her dirty neck and hairline. But her sparkling personality overcame her disheveled appearance.

Luisa came to us laden with necklaces, rings and other trinkets. She jumped into step between us and then propositioned Louise: "This necklace matches your shoes. Make me an offer."

We looked over her offerings, but never found anything of interest. To shut off the chatter, we went to our favorite café for our repast and offered her a Coke. She sat down to drink, but continued her sales pitch.

Louise bought a pair of shoes, which turned out to be one size too small. They fit Luisa perfectly, so Lou gave them to her. The next day, Luisa came to our table wearing her new shoes. She had her vendor-mother in tow. They thanked Louise profusely, but tried to sell nothing, and then went away as they waved to us.

Everyday we passed a beggar who stared forward while holding his left arm aloft. He held his arm in that position all day long. It was purple and marbled with white streaks. There was a bend between his elbow and wrist, which looked like a second elbow that sent his lower arm to his right. His hand and fingernails were gray and looked very dead.

I never gave him anything, because I decided he had a fake arm made of porcelain.

One day, Jim came from his forage of the *mercado* and said, "The guy with the purple arm had his shirt off today. His arm is not a fake."

Thereafter, I put a couple of *pesos* in his tin cup every time I went by him. He continued to stare like a blind man and said nothing. His tin cup usually had nothing in it.

Later, I read in Dr. Andrew Weil's book, *Spontaneous Healing*, a description of this skin disorder. It is a curable disease.

Our hotel featured a half-price (about fifty cents per drink) "Happy Hour." While sipping our margaritas, we spotted two women vendors. They had come to sell us clothes and jewelry. One strode up onto the patio with her full array of things we didn't want.

She was Maria, the mother of six children. She could have been in her twenties, but she looked forty. She spoke to us in Spanish, assuming that if she spoke slowly enough, we would understand. But that didn't work. Her friend, Carmen, was fairly fluent in English. She translated for us when we looked mystified. Carmen had five children, but no husband. Both were attractive and charming ladies.

"Can I buy you ladies margaritas?" I asked.

"*Sí*," they agreed. Maria set her wares down and joined us. Carmen did not come up onto the patio, but spoke from the other side of a concrete fence that surrounded the area. As we savored our drinks, the women took turns telling us about their families. Then the bartender gave Maria the evil eye and a scowl for disturbing customers on the patio, so she joined Carmen on the sidewalk.

When two male vendors joined them, Louise poked me. "Look! The women are hiding their drinks from the men."

It was true. They greeted the men with small talk, holding their drinks behind their backs. When the men disappeared, they picked up their drinks and continued talking.

We saw these women often. They greeted us like old friends, but never tried to sell us anything again.

At breakfast time, a tiny tot came to sell us key chains for five *pesos*. She was bare-footed and had a runny nose, but she was a cherub. I didn't want to haggle with her. I gave her a new twenty *peso* note and she counted out the correct change from a variety of coins that have circulated in Mexico since new coins were minted. The tot knew that the big 1000 *peso* coin was worth only one new *peso*.

"How old are you?" Louise asked in Spanish.

"*Cinco*," she replied.

This five-year-old vendor sold twenty *pesos* worth of trinkets in twenty minutes.

Since these things had been made by prisoners and sold to vendors for one *peso*, her profit was sixteen *pesos*. Compare this with the minimum wage of seventeen *pesos* (about $2.50 at that time) per day for laborers.

Later, we met Fernando, a most engaging salesman. Like Luisa, he was twelve and strictly business. I bought a carved tiger head from him. When he came around later, I told him I really wanted a bigger one, without so many blemishes.

He vanished and came back in five minutes with a big tiger

carved from a reddish-brown wood.

"I'll give you thirty *pesos* and return the old carving for the bigger head," I said.

He looked upward and began writing numbers in the air. He agonized, went through contortions, and said most sadly, "No, no. I must get forty *pesos* extra or I will lose money."

He wrote the number "40" in the sand with his big toe and pleaded for closure on the deal. We settled for 35.

An ancient woman with wrinkles on top of wrinkles hobbled toward us supported by well-worn poles, one of which was longer than the other. She dragged one leg and leaned heavily on both poles as she put her open palm right under our noses and made piteous sounds, presumably asking for money.

As she spoke in a whisper, I noticed that the inside of her mouth was dry and that she had no teeth. Her mouth flapped in and out when she spoke. The skin on her pipe-stem arms was so weathered from the blistering sun that it shone with a brownish-gray cast. We always gave her a few coins worth a nickel or maybe a dime.

One morning, as we ate at the *mercado café*, the old beggar sat at the counter ten feet away and ordered a large Pepsi, an avocado and a roll.

When the proprietor came by, I asked him what her lunch bill came to."

"Two *pesos* (twenty-seven cents)" he replied.

"Please put her lunch on my bill."

When informed, she looked in my direction and waved *gracias* to the big spender. Jim kept looking at the toothless woman, gumming her lunch. And then he asked the proprietor, "How old is she?"

"She's well known in Oaxaca," he replied, "for she will become one hundred next February."

While we shopped around for baskets, Jim contemplated the life this beggar must lead and decided to give her a Christmas gift. He came to me and said, "Do you have a brand new fifty *peso* bill? I'd like to give it to her."

I didn't have one, but I had a perfect 100 *peso* note. Jim, filled with compassion, expounded, "What the hell! Let's give her the whole 100."

He placed the note next to her bottle of Pepsi and said, "*Feliz Navidad.*"

She smiled and thanked Jim.

Two hours later, we saw her striding back to the *Zocalo*, (the town square) like a young gazelle while carrying her two poles in one hand. Later, she accosted Jim with no sign of recognition, rested one pole against her shoulder, held an open hand under his nose and mumbled. She pleaded irresistibly with her watery good eye. What could Jim do? He gave her more money.

HOBBES

Lou yelled across the yard, "Birds are squawking in the shed."
I shouted back, "That must be something else. The baby birds grew up and flew away."

When I approached the shed, the racket sounded like a high-pitched call for help. Scanning the rafters, I couldn't see birds or nests. Following the noise, I lowered my gaze to a deep cardboard box. Inside, four blind kittens quivering in erratic motion meowed with wide-open mouths. They looked like baby birds screeching for worms. The tiny animals looked healthy. They ranged from black-striped, brown-striped to all black. I thought, "Those kittens must belong to the stray cat we saw slinking around the yard the other day."

A warning flashed through my head: "When the grandchildren come, I must tell them not to touch the kittens. Their mother is a wild cat who is afraid of us,' I would say. 'If you leave human smells on them, she might abandon the babies." By the time I remembered to warn them, it was too late! They were already playing with the yowling kittens.

Later that day we saw the mother walk across our deck dragging one leg. She walked laboriously, but disappeared quickly. I bought a bag of cat food and put a bowl of it near the box. For further enticement, I placed pieces of fish and beef in the same dish. I checked hourly. The kittens meowed piteously and the mother cat didn't touch the food. To make it easier for the wounded mother to get into the box, I cut a hole about a foot from the ground. Two days passed and the cat hadn't touched the food. Now the kittens cried softly—their vigor disappeared. When I picked them up they were cold and stiff. The mother must have died from her wound or else abandoned her babies. I took the trembling kittens into the house and put them on quart jars filled with hot water while I warmed some milk. Sensing the heat, they piled on the mason jars. The runt weighed two ounces, the black one, four. The runt still hadn't opened its eyes.

When their bodies were warm and pliable, they began crying again. I tried feeding them milk with an eyedropper, but they wouldn't suck, so we had to force feed them.

Mike, my son-in-law, took the black one home to see if their nursing cat would feed it. That failed, so he brought back a very hungry kitten.

Later, our friends Marie and Gil came to see them. Marie took the black one home but brought it back the next morning. Their cat, George, was so outraged by this intrusion, he stalked out of the house and refused to come home.

Gil explained, "Don't feel bad about Marie bringing the kitten back. If Marie had to make the choice, between George and me, she'd pick the cat every time."

We called the animal shelter for advice. The lady said, "The kittens will not make it on cow's milk. They need more fortified food like *Similac*."

When we went to Safeway, we found a young couple looking at baby food. After seeing how expensive it was, the husband said, "Let's buy one jar to see if the baby likes it."

The wife snatched away that tiny jar of strained beef priced at sixty-nine cents and said, "This baby is going to grow up on free mother's milk of which I have plenty."

My small can of *Similac* cost $2.15.

Since they squirmed and kept climbing, feeding the kittens with an eyedropper was difficult. We solved the problem by restraining them in the same way we had our infants. We wrapped a towel around them so that only their heads stuck out. Once we got the tip of the eyedropper into their mouths, they began sucking. They kept moving their front paws, instinctively trying to knead the mother's breast. The runt of the litter didn't suck and ate very little.

My son-in-law Mike kept calling with tips on the care of kittens. "The mother cat licks the bottoms of the kittens so that they can urinate and defecate."

Later I heard him describing our phone call to his neighbor. He chuckled. "And there was a long pause on the other end. Then he said, 'I guess these kittens will get all bound up and die.'"

My seven-year-old granddaughter came to my rescue.

"Wipe their bottoms with a wet rag until they piddle and poop," she suggested.

This became the routine five times a day. We wiped the bottoms of squirming kittens over the sink while they peed and defecated. The feces were yellow and about the diameter of a fine pencil lead. Like dedicated parents of quadruplets, we took care of our new family.

We tried to determine the gender by looking at their genitals. They all looked alike. The photos in the cat book didn't help. Our knowledgeable granddaughter looked at the rear ends of all four and declared that the black was a female and the others males. Not trusting her skills, we asked a retired biology professor to have a look. She had been correct. The biologist added, "Females have two holes."

Word about our kittens spread. Alma, the tennis teacher, came to visit the tiny patients. When she picked one up, it fell asleep. She whispered, "I can't leave until it wakes up. I think they need a nursing bottle with a nipple." She drove to Cenex ten miles away and brought back the bottle. We enlarged the hole until the formula dripped easily. In a couple of days, the kittens learned to suck milk out of the bottle.

At night, they crapped all over one another. Maybe the runt had diarrhea. They needed a washing down every morning. The mother cat would have licked them clean. Cat lovers came to examine the litter. One couple selected two. Lou made the generous offer, "Take any two you want." When the woman, whose name was "Bev," chose the one with the brown face, Lou cried, "Not that one. We've already named him Hobbes! You know, the tiger in *Calvin and Hobbes*." So Bev obligingly picked the one with the black-and-white face and "Blackie," leaving me Hobbes and the ailing runt. The next day, the runt gave its last shiver and died.

We learned from the vet that the feed store sold a special formula for kittens. The yellow powder cost about eleven dollars a pound. Bev's black-and-white and our Hobbes became listless and too weak to stand up. We exchanged progress reports several times a day with Bev. And we hovered over those kittens and fed them a few drops often so they wouldn't dehydrate. They were sick for three days, and then recovered. The vet guessed that switching from Similac to the formula had caused the problem.

Lou had to leave town for a seminar, so Bev called to invite me for dinner. Bev's husband suggested, "Bring your cat so the brothers and sister can have a reunion." The three of us sprawled on the floor to see what they would do. Hobbes ran to one, touched noses, and did the same with the other. After wrestling around, they piled into a heap and went to sleep. After dinner, I left Hobbes with them to have a slumber party. When I picked him up, two days later, he had gained one ounce. That's a seventeen percent growth in two days.

The next day, Alma (the tennis teacher) rapped on my door breathless with good news. Before she could say anything, her dog, Charlie, bounded into the house and began licking Hobbes who was sitting in the middle of the room. The dog, a mixture of Australian Dingo and Alaskan Husky, was a formidable beast. Before I gathered my senses to save Hobbes, Charlie had him in his mouth. When I rescued the wet animal, Charlie put his jowls on my lap and stared at me with eyes of two different colors, gray and blue. While I went through my gyrations of panic, Alma watched with no visible concern. She explained, "Charlie did the same thing with our kitten. He wouldn't hurt him. He was mothering."

In spite of the enormous odds, brave Hobbes hissed at Charlie.

Alma took the kitten and stroked it while she told me her wonderful news: "There's a cat swollen with milk. Her owner has just given away her littler of kittens and would like to give away the mother."

Alma was crestfallen that I didn't jump up and down with joy. "I don't want two cats," I said. "We already tried to get another mother cat to nurse the black one, but the mother rejected it."

Later that day, Jim Westall dropped by and watched me feed my pet with a nursing bottle. He saw me wipe the kitten's rear and then let the kitten climb my pant legs and onto my lap. He observed, "You're going to have a neurotic cat."

"You mean because he'll imprint on me?"

"He thinks you're his mother."

"I'm behaving like his mother."

At four in the morning, I began thinking perhaps Alma's proposal had merit. I tossed it around, waiting for a reasonable hour to call her. Seven-thirty was the latest I could stand, and I woke her up.

"Do you think the mother cat is still full of milk?" I asked. "I think my kitten should have a normal life with a real cat mother."

"Of course she is," Alma replied. "Here's the phone number. I'll drive you out."

The house was thirty miles away, in the boondocks of Hood Canal. We looked for the tavern where the cat lived. A closed sign greeted us, but a friendly neighbor said, "Dee opens at twelve."

Looking around the yard, we saw a big source of cat milk going to waste. She ignored us, and we didn't feel like scaling an eight-foot high fence to grab our treasure.

The tavern opened. The cat we were thinking of stealing was the wrong one. The one we wanted was a gray giant, but she didn't acknowledge my tiny animal. In spite of her indifference to my kitten, we took Mouse Trap (M.T.) home. M. T. climbed to the top of the stairs and growled. I put her on my lap and directed Hobbes mouth toward a teat. It had been so long since sucking on the real article, he failed to find one even when I put his mouth right up to a luscious teat. After many false starts, he finally found one and sucked happily. M. T. began struggling and freed herself. When the kitten tried to get under the cat, she growled and moved away. She had no use for Hobbes. Hobbes scampered away from the ferocious M. T. and climbed on top of my shoe for safety.

Too bad. Hobbes would have to make do with me as a mother figure. We could face the world as Carl and Hobbes.

While I was feeling sorry for us, Alma called with yet another suggestion. "The plumber working on our water system has a cat with a litter of five. He's willing to let your kitten join the family."

I scooped up Hobbes, picked up Alma and went to Jeff's trailer. When Alma put my kitten in front of the big mama, she started to give him a thorough cleaning, including his rear end. When I put his mouth right up to the biggest teat in the rear, he didn't know what to do. The inexperienced orphan climbed to the top of the cat. On the fourth try, he discovered what he was supposed to do. When a husky orange kitten tried to buck him out of position, Hobbes hung on by making himself a powerful suction cup.

Jeff promised, "If the mother cat rejects your kitten, I'll call."

Hobbes came home six weeks later with bright eyes that were free from matter, his wounds healed, and his fur grown back over the sore sites. He had become a happy cat.

JOB JAR

For over thirty-five years, it was a battle of wits. Louise figured out tasks for me to do and put them in the "job jar." I made it a point to ignore them. These tasks, also known as "honey do," did not actually exist in a jar, but on a list indelibly imprinted in Louise's head. Though I turned down my hearing aid, I knew what was on the list because she refreshed my memory often by reciting the hateful chores.

As the list aged, Lou's expectations declined so that anything I did, however poorly, appeared wonderful. This became the standard operating procedure. For example, Louise lusted after shelves next to the pantry door. Three years and many dozens of reminders later, I made the shelves in a few minutes with scrap wood. The workmanship drew scorn from friends, but Louise was thrilled to get those crummy shelves.

It seemed so easy to hire someone to do those tasks. Why did she insist on my doing them? It was persecution. Maybe her Depression Years' mentality dictated that we couldn't afford it. Maybe it was her ingrained belief that "busy hands are happy hands." That was true for her. But I'm made of different stuff. My hands are gloriously happy without chores like that.

One year, she ran into a fantastic stroke of good luck. It happened after a fund-raising slave auction at church. The idea was that members offered their services for sale and the church kept the proceeds. I signed a ticket with the agreement that I would work for eight hours for anyone, doing any kind of grunt work.

We bid silently by holding up a white card indicating agreement to pay whatever price the auctioneer was quoting at the moment. The auctioneer started me (as a slave) at twenty dollars, which quickly rose to twenty-five. The bids started jumping up in increments of ten dollars until the highest bidder got me for ninety-five dollars. That was an amazing rate for my marginal skills. I wondered what millionaire was willing to pay that much for me.

There was much tittering within the audience and finally applause for the winning bidder. My wife, sitting a few rows behind me, had me at last. Simon Legree found a solution to her overstuffed "Job Jar."

MY MOTHER MIZUKO'S DEATH

After the war, Mizuko lived mostly with Yosh, but her children hovered around her. And her twenty grandchildren adored their kindly grandmother. At the age of ninety-one, in 1986, she died, leaving her legacy of hardship and abuse by a cruel husband behind her.

Nevertheless, she emerged a kind and gentle person. She was a great mother! It is a pity that she married such a selfish and brutal man just because she was too tall and she wanted to escape from a cruel stepmother. She could have been a doctor, married well and lived an untroubled life in Japan. The good news is that none of us beat our children as Kazuichi had beaten us.

CHAPTER XI

Life After Louise

MY EULOGY FOR LOUISE

September 3, 1997

Minneapolis, Minnesota

Thank you for coming to this memorial. We are honoring Louise Nomura who died last Sunday in an automobile accident. You have come forth with overwhelming support and love for her and concern for my well being. You have given me your condolences and hundreds of hugs. Lou always avoided the limelight. She would have been astounded by your response.

Last Thursday, the community of Port Townsend organized a similar memorial. An amazing 600 people (some counted 700-750) came to say goodbye to her. Four newspaper articles have appeared in local newspapers. AAUW named its scholarship after Louise.

Life is so fragile. In one moment she was a happy and vital person and, without notice, she left. I can't believe it. Many times a day I expect to see her coming down the stairs or calling me for a meal. I find myself saying things like, "Lou, look what Suzie sent us."

During the last week of her life, we attended two family reunions: first with our nuclear family and Louise's cousin, and then the big Nomura reunion at a retreat and conference center near Portland, Oregon. Louise taught a host of children water coloring, she played tennis, swam, and then beat everyone in scrabble and gin rummy. She interacted with the seventy friends and relatives who were there.

On the second day, we had an intergenerational program to introduce one another. She was asked, "What would you wish for if you could be granted anything you wanted?"

Without hesitation, Louise answered, "Nothing. I have everything I want or ever wanted, and I have done everything I wanted to do. I'm a 'play girl'! Life is wonderful!"

She left the reunion early to finish her sculpture that needed more work. Besides, she didn't want to eat Chinese food. But before she got into the car, the whole gathering came out to give her a hug. She put her arms around me and said happily, "I'll see you at home."

That was the last time we saw her alive.

In just three more months we would have reached our fiftieth anniversary. She had looked forward to that event. On our forty-ninth, we stayed in the honeymoon suite at a fancy Port Townsend hotel. We arrived so late that the restaurant had closed. Our anniversary dinner was two slices of pizza and coffee at McDonald's. This reminded both of us of our wedding night. Then we were so poor that our dinner was Limburger cheese and Ritz crackers.

But none of that bothered Louise. She was gutsy, loving, competitive, independent and fiercely outspoken. She once said to a visitor we had not seen for several years, "Boy, you got old!"

Her last act of defiance was to shoot me down when I interviewed for the Peace Corps. Six months before, she had agreed to go to the interview with me and be supportive. But during the two months I had to wait for an appointment, she changed her mind. Her exercising buddies told her it was a dumb idea, that I would get some jungle disease and die.

"Don't let him go," one of them said.

Unfortunately, she didn't let me in on her change of heart. So when the day came for the interview, I took her with me. The interviewer asked me, "How's your health?"

"I'm fine," I replied. "Never better."

"No he's not," Louise interrupted. "He's a near-diabetic, he's blind, he must have Alzheimers Disease because he can't remember anything, he's arthritic, and besides he has gout. I don't want to go. I don't want him to do it."

And throughout the interview she continued to give disruptive answers to questions directed at me. Finally, I said, "Let me answer those questions because he's asking me and not you."

With her testimonials, I could not have landed a job as a peanut vendor.

Two weeks later, the interviewer told me, "I sent your unusual case to our head office in Washington, D.C. You could have been assigned anytime at any place in the world because there are hundreds of failing small businesses that need your expertise. But we can't take you. We are not in the business of breaking up marriages."

Upon hearing this devastating verdict, Louise just beamed and showed not the slightest trace of contrition for her sabotage.

I'm pleased to report that she died with no regrets and knowing that she was loved by a host of people. She had the satisfaction of seeing her children grow into responsible and good people, and she cherished her grandchildren. Family, friends, art and the well being of our small church Fellowship were central to her life. Now she is gone, but memories of her will remain. I am sure that, at her last moment, she said to her self, "That was a good life."

DEALING WITH LOSS

How do you recover from that kind of loss? Very slowly, as I have discovered. First of all, you accept every invitation, for it keeps you from having too much time to think. Keep very busy and you may survive the pain. And you try to learn new things. That also occupies the mind.

And then, when you do think, try to be positive. This is a partial quote from a Christmas letter I wrote two months after Louise's death:

December 20, 1997

Greetings!

'It was the best of times, it was the worst of times...'
C. Dickens,

'Now what?' C. Nomura

Very often, Louise would say, 'I don't fear death. It just happens to be the last step in life. I have done everything I wanted to do and received every thing I've wanted. Life is wonderful. I have no regrets.'

She was guileless, for she had no secrets including yours if you had confided in her. She blurted out anything that came to mind, such as, 'Boy, you got fat.'

She lived every day as though it were her last, an idea I think she learned from Aristotle. And I never saw her so happy as she was in those last months. At the family reunion, she kidded everyone and later hammed it up on the stage. Then she died, not quietly, but by running into an oncoming truck in a fifty-mile-per-hour zone and tying up traffic for four hours. She was the only casualty.

And suddenly I was alone for the first time in almost fifty years. For two months, I wrote about 800 'thank you' letters while answering anguished phone calls. I know I missed many of you, so please accept my gratitude via this letter for your condolences, attending her memorials, sending cards, letters and notes, and mailing gifts to her memorial. The Quimper Unitarian Universalist Fellowship Building Fund has now exceeded the astounding figure of $13,000. Many of you also contributed toward the Louise Nomura AAUW Scholarship Endowment as well as to your own churches.

In the meantime, I have asked for suggestions about how I should live. Many of you responded and others have volunteered ideas. Here are some of them:

1. Don't make any changes for six to twelve months.
2. Don't give away or sell Louise's things. (She was little, but she consumed 75 percent of our communal space and 90 percent of the closets and drawers.)
3. Accept every invitation, no matter what. (Do you really mean every?)
4. Don't rush into a relationship. (What's a relationship?)
5. If it feels right, get into a relationship. (How far can I trust my feelings?)
6. Watch out for bad women who try to take away your money. (What money?)
7. VDs (Venereal Disease) are rampant in the 90's, so watch out! (Not new. I saw those 'watch out' movies in the Army.)
8. Don't play hard to get. (Not very likely.)
9. Write your specs for a mate. (What? To get married again?)
10. Follow your instincts.
11. Do what your heart tells you to do.

Some of the suggestions you gave are wise, some look like lots of fun, while others appear to invite disaster. What to do? I like 'follow your instincts' and 'do what the heart says.' Yes, I'll do both, but still try to be rational.

The only notable event for me was supposed to happen on March 14th, *Pi* Day: 3-14. Get it? On that day, the odometer on my Ford Ranger would have registered 31,415.9, which is *Pi* taken to six significant figures. Before leaving for my vacation, I left instructions that nobody was to drive that truck. But somebody did drive it and overshot the coveted *Pi* reading. I wept. I didn't want to run that Ford backward for 112.3 miles.

Teri restored my happiness by buying a VW speedometer from a junkyard and resetting the odometer to *Pi* with an electric drill. What a great seventy-fifth birthday present! I also got a personalized license plate for my car with 3.1416. What else would you expect from a *Pi* nut?

In the meantime I am studying poetry under the guidance of a teacher. With my newfound knowledge, I now understand why I never understood poetry. Maybe I'll crank out a poetic letter next year.

I also plan to take cello lessons. I'll retire when I begin to sound like Yo Yo Ma playing a Brahms' Concerto.

I'll make trips to Greece and to Japan with some of my grandchildren. For next summer we are also planning a nuclear family reunion at Camp Unistar in Cass Lake, Minnesota. I'm in great health. The kids hover over me to make sure I stay that way. My friends continue to take care of me, so I live in the lap of luxury and good will.

DEATH AND DYING

Someone suggested I get some grief counseling, and, having as hard a time as I was, in those first months after Louise died, it seemed like a good idea. I couldn't sleep, and I was like a walking zombie. I made an appointment with a psychologist. She helped me learn to live with my loss, and also pointed out the necessity of planning for my own death. I had, in fact, already written a letter of instruction to Lou and the children, for I had always assumed I would die first. Now it was time to revise that letter and address it to my children. Here it is:

Dear Kathi, Teri, John and Dave,

'You must have instructions for your family in the event that you become terminally ill or die,' advised Dr. Maggie Jamison, a psychologist who gives counsel to the dying and to grieving survivors. She added, 'If you do not, you'll leave a mess that will frustrate everyone. Save them the onerous task of guessing and sleuthing.' You must know what I want done and where the records are of the property, investments, living will, other legal documents, my commitments, commitments to me by others, insurance policies, who were important to me, etc.

Today I am perfectly sane (in fact, absolutely sane), balanced and in very good health. Dr. Jamieson inspired me to write this document while in this condition. This will assure you that these instructions are valid. Since I will be out of control, incapacitated, or dead, you may choose to alter these requests. But I'd appreciate it if you would carry them out.

During the past year, Bernice Johanson, Pete Wargo, Jim Bottomley, Vance Lewton, Helen Katagiri, Van Bearinger, Ted Melvin, and my brother Henry died. I gave the eulogy at one service, spoke at two others, and Marcia Lewton asked me to be a speaker at Vance's service, which I was unable to attend. With great certainty, many others of my friends will follow in rapid succession since my friends are approaching or are now advanced senior citizens. Since I am not immortal, although I behave as though I am, someday I will die. Life is very fragile.

I don't fear death because I have few regrets. I have done most of the things I wanted to do and I will continue doing them as long as I can. In the Aristotelian sense, as I expel my last breath, I expect to look back at my life and assert, 'That was a good life.'

I have tons of friends whom I cherish. My family is great! The kids turned out well and the grandchildren are turning out equally well. I am so grateful that they rally around me. My work was tough, but rewarding.

Recently, Jim Westall asked, 'What would you do differently if you had your life to live over?' The answer to this question would be a summary of my regrets. I would listen closely to what the children were saying to me and I would be more affectionate.

What to Do if I Become Terminally Ill

Do no heroics to save me. No transfusions, no tubes, no force-feeding, no antibiotics or anything else that keeps me alive as a gelatinous blob. I want the right to pull my own plug when I choose to do so. Don't grieve because I've just entered an inevitable and natural phase of life. It just happens to be the last one. I came, I did, and now I'm going. I won't grieve and neither should you.

Let me clarify what I mean by no heroics to save me. It begins when I am no longer able to take care of myself in normal activities such as eating, eliminating, walking, bathing, etc. It is a condition when I would be a burden to someone whether it be a member of the family or a hired person.

It furthermore is a condition when my quality of life is so degraded that there is no joy. If I should reach such a condition, don't keep me alive with drugs, tubes, machines or any such life supporting or sustaining means. A good criterion is this: if I'm helpless for three months, then forget life supporting aids. Remember, I've lived and done all the things I wanted to do. If I should choose to stop eating or drinking, then so be it. Allow me.

What to Do When I Die

When I die, four things will have to be done:

> Get rid of the body
> Organize memorial services
> Interpret the will
> File insurance claims

Teri (or Dave as alternate) as executor of the estate, will begin managing the assets to complete instructions given in the will. Keep things simple. Don't have a viewing of the body. Give the body to the University of Washington or to a hospital for parts or whatever they wish to do with the cadaver. If they insist on returning some of the remains, have them cremated. If nobody wants the body, cremate it and bring back none of the ashes, for they have no place to go. If I should die away from home, have the body cremated locally. If you have a problem with my indifference to the ashes, have someone spread them under the great tree, 'Unifir,' or on the shores of Lake

Windigo where I had such wonderful times.

I wish no headstone because I consider cemeteries a waste of land, a burden to society and an ugly defacement to the earth. A far better memorial is to have a gathering of my friends who could relive the great times we had together. Have two events, one in Port Townsend, and the other at the First Unitarian Society in Minneapolis. From my computer address list, use the Washington addresses for the Washington friends, the Minnesota addresses for my Minnesota friends.

Do not involve anyone in the service who didn't know me. I witnessed a meaningless charade several years ago at a church on Bainbridge Island. It was a memorial service for a woman who had lived on the island fifty years before. A minister who didn't know the woman gave the eulogy by comparing her with Moses. He held forth about Moses for twenty minutes and said almost nothing about the woman. Keep such strangers off the stage, for they just take up time and address none of the things that were important to the deceased.

Invite my friends to meet one another, for it has always pleased me to see my friends getting to know one another. Encourage them to speak about whatever they wish. Hopefully, they will tell about our wonderful lives together. Have a joke telling contest. Ask them to bring good things to eat and drink, for I love parties.

If people want to send money, advise them that, since our friends contributed so generously to Louise's memorial, ask them not to send any more money. They have done enough for both of us. Ask them not to send flowers for my soul. I'm more impressed with relationships and people's achievements than I am about the perfection and wonders of nature. If questioned, recite the following story:

Lady: "Aren't the clarions beautiful?"
Me: "Can't hear you lady. The damned bells are making too much noise."

Play *Pomp and Circumstance* by Edward Elgar in recognition of my great moment, the Van Nuys High School commencement of winter, 1941. So that people will understand the relevance of this music, have someone read my essay entitled *Pomp and Circumstance*.

Play Mozart with Yo Yo Ma holding forth on the cello. Get live music. Have my singer friends sing. Play Beethoven's *Ninth Symphony*. Have Nelson Eddy and Jeanette McDonald blast out *Ah Sweet Mystery of Life* or *I'm Falling In Love with Someone*. Play *Stardust*. Play Brahms' *Violin Concerto*, the passages where the cello has solos.

Several people have asked me, 'Aren't you concerned about the hereafter?' No, I am not. It is my opinion that when I die, that's the end. *Finis!* There is no more, but it has been a great life!

With love,
Dad

PHILOSOPHY OF LIFE

The primary purpose of my life is to enjoy to the fullest all of the goodness that life has to offer me. My aspiration is to become a self-actualized person by being as good and competent as I can be while pursuing happiness.

To realize these ends, whenever I reach a decision point on something important to me, I always choose the path that gives me growth in some way or that does good for someone else. In my relationships with people, I am a Pollyanna since I assume that people are good and trustworthy. The obvious exceptions are the deranged and corrupt ones who don't know the difference between right and wrong.

Being kind to others gives me a more harmonious life while improving my relationships with people. I also try to be modest even though I stumble from time to time. I have used these ideas in managing organizations, and the results have been good. Kindness also worked out very well for me in marriage.

Health

For the attainment of the good life described above, I need both good physical and mental health. Therefore, I will maintain physical health through proper diet, exercise and a low-stress lifestyle. For mental health, I will pursue both knowledge and skills as follows:

1. Learn or listen to three languages: Japanese, Spanish and Latin.

2. Read at least 1,500 books, some of which are the classics, math, physics, biology, psychology, philosophy, and the aesthetics.

3. Become skilled in duplicate bridge, poker, tennis, the computer, horticulture, and woodworking.

4. Write and publish at least three books that will have an acceptably wide readership, and learn about and write some publishable poetry.

5. The three books now in process concern life stories, management and higher geometric curves.
6. Learn enough music so that I am able to understand and appreciate the Western classics.

Family

I will love and cherish my children and their offspring. I will invest time and other resources for their well-being. Should the need arise, they may have any of my material possessions, including my body parts.

Friends

I will nurture and be loyal to my friends. Though most of my friends in the past were men, I may now expand that to include women since I am single and will no longer be constrained by societal rules for married men. Among my friends, there will be a special woman who I will love and honor.

Financial Independence

Through good income and asset management, I will have enough money to do whatever I please, get whatever I want, and not be a burden to my family or my friends if I should become disabled.

Fellow Man

At the age of twenty, I made it my mission to work for the cause of the persecuted and other marginalized members of society. To be effective, I concluded that I needed enough education to know what to do, and enough achievements so that people would pay heed.

Beliefs

One of the basic tenets of many religions is to believe in God, something supernatural or a higher being, because we have many "unknowables" that are beyond our comprehension. Indeed, the Pope advises cosmologists not to probe too deeply. I believe that in time, say 500 or 1,000 years, these "unknowables" will be whittled down to an insignificant few because of our exponential expansion of knowledge about everything. We will even resolve the questions of how the universe and life began. I, therefore, place no reliance for solace on anything or anyone supernatural.

LADY

Jim Westall came to my house with a doberman pincer in tow. He asked, "Will you keep this dog for a few days until I find a home for it? She belongs to a lady who found her at the animal shelter. She has a useless front leg that she drags around. A dog that size should weigh about seventy pounds, but she's only about thirty-five. Audrey felt so sorry for her that she took it to a vet to have the leg removed and her health restored. It cost $2,500. Then, when she brought the doberman home, the other housedog rejected her so fiercely that Audrey decided she had to find a home for her. I volunteered to help."

Several days later, Audrey came to visit her dog.

"What's her name?" I asked. "And how old is she?"

"It's 'Lady,' and she's six and a half years old. Here are her health records, feeding and watering bowls, some bones that she likes, and a toy that she ignores. You also need to trim her toenails because Lady doesn't run around enough to wear them down."

"What was wrong with her leg?"

"It was cancer. So the leg had to be removed at the shoulder. She's a sweetie, and maybe I'm giving you the better of my two dogs."

After meeting her other dog, I had to agree.

Before leaving, she hugged Lady and kissed her on the mouth. Obviously this was a loved dog. I called Jim and told him I'd be keeping Lady. He gave a huge sigh of relief.

Unlike most Dobermans, Lady still had untrimmed ears. So they stood tall and made her look like a deer. When she was happy, she'd wag her one-inch stub of a tail. From long practice, she ran well with only three legs. She had an extra back leg kick she did when she ran, but I was able to out-run her.

She must have been abused, because she cowered if I reached forward to pet her. But she had impeccable manners. For example, she never gobbled her food. She ate only when I told her it was okay. She also pooped by backing into a bush. When she came into the house, she didn't wander around, chew the furniture or dirty the room. She stayed in one corner of the living room. She obeyed all the commands such as "Come," "Stay," "Down," and "Sit," but she would not "Heel." And I couldn't teach her to shake hands. She needed that front paw to support herself. I loved that dog, so I gave her about five hugs a day. In time she quit cowering and smiled often.

When I took her for our daily three-mile walks at the beach or at Ft. Worden, I turned her loose. She liked to run ahead for a hundred feet or so and then turn, pass me and run a hundred feet to my back. We always encountered other strollers with their dogs. One was a fierce doberman with trimmed ears who always snarled at us and strained at his chain. In the meantime, my Lady would hang out her tongue and laugh. So I teased the owner of the vicious dog. "My dog is happier than your dog." She agreed.

Lady became so bonded to me that she followed me everywhere and ignored other people. When I returned from a trip, the house and dog-sitter said, "Every day while you were gone, whenever I drove into the yard, Lady would come running out. But when she saw that it was only me, she'd turn around and go into her dog house."

After having her for a year and a half, I found out that her kidneys failed. The vet said there was no cure. She suffered for seven days and, just before drawing her last breath, this wonderful pet strained forward to lick my hand.

CHRISTMAS LETTER (DECEMBER 10, 1998)

Thanks again for your generosity and for canon-
izing Louise a saint. Your contributions to her
memorial totaled $14,000. One thousand dol-
lars went to an AAUW scholarship that is ear-
marked this year for a woman working toward a
master's degree. The rest will be used for a memorial courtyard at the Quimper Unitarian Universalist Fellowship that will accommodate 120
people. Its shape was inspired by fractals, those
infinitely diminishing and replicating figures that
were described on the PBS channel last year. The
courtyard is somewhat circular and leads to several similarly shaped, but smaller, satellite enclo-
sures, one of which is a meditation garden with a
flowing fountain at its far end. All will be surrounded by vegetation.

I cut off the branches from six scraggly apple
trees and had a man do 140 bark grafts on those
stumps with twenty-five scab-free varieties. The
herd of Bambis that roam freely around my yard
demolished about forty, but the rest look good.
I'll have fruits from June through November.
Come visit me then to eat the apples of the season. My figs, kiwis, cherries, apricots, plums,
peaches, grapes, walnuts, pears, filberts, blueber-
ries and strawberries will be sensational. I will not
starve. Neither will the deer, raccoons, robins,

blackbirds and my frugivorous friends.

I'm building a chicken house. I'll get those hens that lay blue eggs and some Minorcas that lay giant ones. To the horror of my anti-vivisectionist and vegetarian friends, I intend to caponize (fix) the roosters. They will not crow and will grow big and succulent. Those rascals will be happy and have free-range of a half-acre yard. I will not give them names such as Harvey, George, et. al. I'll call them Chick, Soup, Roast or Drumstick.

I composed my first Shakespearean style sonnet. It is perfect technically but so exceedingly boring that I will not show it to you. I have a new respect for the bard who wrote so much wonderful stuff in iambic pentameter. Structured poetry is far more difficult than theoretical physics. Progress is slow because my teacher is so incredibly beautiful that I stare at her and barely hear what she is saying. Such is the plight of dirty old men, but what a great trade-off.

I decided to forget the cello. I don't have four hours a day to burn for practicing and besides I have an aching joint on my A string finger. Instead, I'll concentrate on getting my book of homely stories published. The greatest challenge will be to keep my computer from dying (at this moment I can't print or make copies on this *#@^> machine.)

I'm now able to come and go as I please, because I have a live-in gardener and house sitter who lives in what used to be Louise's studio. It has been converted to an apartment. My yard looks like the Garden of Versailles and is free of weeds. I learned recently on the Internet that old men like to talk about lawn mowers. To fit that stereotype, I report that I love my Honda 2013 riding tractor. It makes a carpet out of my one-acre lawn in an hour.

I'm continuing my project of taking grand-children on vacations. Last July I took two grand-daughters to Greece. Next year, I'll take five more kids to Japan and the Galapagos Islands. In between I'll do some Elderhosteling, cruising and fishing in Alaska and Ontario. When I'm hanging around at home, I have a great social life with ladies, visiting local friends, bridge, poker, tennis, language studies and hosting dinners. Visit me while I still have most of my marbles and be full of p— and vinegar, but come when I'm home!

With much love,
Carl Nomura

*Garrison Keillor once described the process when he discovered infinity: the picture of the girl holding a round box of Morton salt has her picture holding a small box of salt. On that box is a still small picture of the same girl holding a round box of Morton salt, and so on, *ad infinitum.*

CHRISTMAS LETTER (NOVEMBER 24, 1999)

Thirty years ago, a fur-lined toilet seat seemed to me both kinky and needlessly luxurious. But over the years, my tastes have advanced toward greater creature comforts. The first step in this trend toward decadence was my installation of a high-tech, heated toilet seat. It is equipped with a jet that aims warm water to wash me and, when I am squeaky clean, a fan blows me dry. I can control the jet pressure, the water temperature, and even make it pulsate. Whee! There's also a bidet with the same range of controls. Think of the money I'm saving on toilet paper! The bathroom is now my recreation center, so there is almost no reason for me to go out for entertainment. This hydraulic marvel fills me with patriotism for a reason I attribute to Napoleon Bonaparte, who declared, 'A nation with a clean crotch is a strong nation.'

The second step toward decadence was the purchase of a feather mattress. When I lie on it, I sink and become tucked in just as my mother used to do. When ensconced in my goose down cocoon, with the down comforter over me, I disappear. It is so pleasant I am finally overcoming my insomnia.

For a couple of years, I have been playing Luther Burbank by grafting all kinds of things on my plants. I have twenty-five varieties of apples on five trees, and six kinds of Asian pears on three trees, two of them being Hawthornes which bear nothing but fungus infested leaves. Its only saving grace is that it belongs to the pear family and will accept pear grafts. I tried grafting tomatoes on potato plants and got a couple of tomatoes as well as spuds. Grafting potatoes on tomato plants produced nothing. This is as purposeless as a solar-powered flashlight I read about in the book, *Useless Inventions.*

This year I advanced from Sr. Citizenhood to old geezerhood when my daughter, Kathi, called to say, "Wish me Happy Birthday! Today I became fifty."

I said, "I didn't want to know that."

But time marches on and the parts do wear out. I had so many things done to my teeth and eyes that last year I thought a better solution was a head transplant. I'd get thirty-two perfect teeth, 20/20 vision, good looks and an uncluttered brain. Now it looks like I need everything under the head. For example, prostate cancer gets about 50 percent of the men by age seventy and 100 percent by eighty. I am a victim of this malady. Though the National Cancer Institute advises no treatment for men over seventy, I took PC Spec, a mixture of Chinese herbs that caused my PSA to plunge from 4.7 to .38 in just ten weeks. I'm impressed with the wisdom of the ancient Chinese herbalists.

To cheer me up and to make sure I had at least one friend, Kathi gave me a Border Collie pup for fathers' day. I named him Bravo after Charles Darwin's dog. Bravo took charge immediately. I became his pet and learned to heel, sit and come. We are going to puppy obedience school now so that I can become the alpha dog and Bravo the obedient follower and gamma dog.

I'll not write about my fantastic, still-married children and their brilliant kids, my fabulous vacations, fancy car, and exciting social life. If you want to hear about them, come visit me. I'll give you an 800-slide presentation in dazzling Kodacolor, or I'll serve tea and cookies, or maybe martinis.

FLOWERS

(A Ghazal[4])

Neglected, desiccated, sorrowful Jade Plant,
Unlike its sisters, majestic with white blooms.
Oxalis, green and like giant shamrocks and
Purple ones, asleep, folded, with bright blooms.
Gangly, serpentine, night blooming ceres,
Whose grandeur goes unnoticed with night blooms.
Four-way plum, dominating with spectacular beauty,
Summer's cornucopia transformed from selenite blooms.
Succulent figs, apples, cherries for robins and deer.
A few left over for Carl who worships eye-bright blooms.

Epilogue

When King Lear became four score years old, Shakespeare described him as "worn with age"—so that he might have time to prepare for death. When I became eighty, I had no such moribund thoughts. Instead, when I wake up each morning I visualize a dozen things I want to do. They might be to practice Spanish, pick pears, try to solve an integral calculus problem, plant seeds for a winter crop, write an essay, write a few letters, wash clothes, simmer corned beef for dinner with friends, clean off my desk—. Though busy, life is a bowl of cherries. I am able to do these things, yet I agree that parts do wear out and don't work as well as they did in the past.

On the topic of death, far from contemplating it, I live as though I am immortal. Indeed, I made a list of ten things I want to accomplish before I die and then asked Lois Twelves to marry me. To my surprise, the things I wrote down on this list are almost identical to the things I listed for my "physical and mental health" list earlier in this book. But I want to list them here again, because my life has dramatically changed since I composed my first list, so naturally, some of my goals changed to the following in descending order of importance:

1. Make my marriage with Lois successful.

2. Maximize my health through proper diet, exercise, supplements, pursuit of knowledge, laugh often, and maintain good relations with my family and friends.

3. Transfer all assets to the kids so they will have minimal tax liabilities and that I will be penniless when I finally expire.

4. Read 1,500 books of substance. Assuming that I live until I'm ninety-five, the rate will be about two books a week.

5. Publish three books with reasonable public acceptance. I expect *Sleeping on Potatoes* will be the first of these. I've started my second book entitled, *Successful Management with Low Stress.*

6. Learn Spanish, Japanese and Latin well enough to read books in their native languages. For starters, they will be Gabriel Marquez' *100 Years of Solitude*, Natsume Soseki's *Botchan* and Sir Isaak Newton's *Mathematical Principles of Natural Philosophy.*

7. Become proficient in poker, bridge, math, physics, dancing, and gardening. For math and physics, some of them will be relearning things I once
knew. I'm refreshing just like random access
memories do in computers.

8. Continue to travel abroad at least twice a year.

9. Learn option trading well enough to make it worth
my while.

10. Learn classical music sufficiently so that I can understand why I like it, especially the music of
Brahms, Mozart and Beethoven.

While I was a bachelor for five years after Louise's death, I
met many women and I decided I liked Lois Twelves the best. In
the old fashioned way, I got down on my knees and asked her to
marry me. She contemplated the proposal and then said, "Yes."
My neighbor, Anne, walked in while I was proposing but backed
out of the house quickly. She knew what was going on.

Teri made the wedding dress, which drew raves. We staged
the wedding outdoors at the Nomura family reunion in Portland,
Oregon. Lois' family and a few close friends came from Washington, Oregon and California. We composed the ceremony and the
leading promise was that we would accept each other just as we
are. When I read it leisurely, it took only 2.5 minutes so we had
three grandchildren and a grandnephew play Bach and Brahms as
a string quartet and then Lois' daughter, Gail, volunteered to sing
the *Lord's Prayer*. It still was too short so we asked Tim Haley, the
minister, to add some "boiler plate" to stretch it out to about fif-

teen minutes. We were eating cake within thirty minutes. Amazingly, the guests consumed the whole wedding cake.

For our Port Townsend and Seattle friends, we had a reception at the church where we had catered both Japanese and Scandinavian foods. The caterer dubbed the combination of Sushi and *Krum Kake* "Japanavian " food. Over 200 came to give us their blessings.

For a honeymoon, we went to Nootka Island Lodge in Northern Vancouver Island to fish for Salmon. We caught thirteen King and Coho Salmons weighing a total of 225 pounds. We brought home filets and shared them with about fifty of our friends. We had a triple hitter. Each of the three events was a four-star event.

For my eightieth birthday, Teri organized a big party with a committee of workers. They sent invitations to my entire Christmas card list of about 700 addresses. It was supposed to be a secret but a ninety-four year-old gent spilled the beans by saying to me: "Thanks for inviting me to your secret birthday party." About 300 came to the blast that featured dozens of balloons and giant cranes since I'm an *Origami* nut. There were many cakes and two of them were square apple pies made by Joanna England and Will Young that had the caption: "Pi are square." Jim Westall hosted the event and was the M.C. About fifteen people went on stage to tell stories about me. Some were moving but there were several outlandish ones.

Since people were asked to send in stories about me, hundreds of them came in. Teri compiled them into three, 3.5-inch thick notebooks. It took me three days to read the ten-inch stack. I read them a second time because people kept asking me, -What did you think about what I wrote to you?" There are touching stories but they are too numerous to cite, so I will choose three; two of them were from men who wrote about their childhood experiences with me and the third from a woman who worked for me as an executive secretary.

Story One: Kyle McKeen was my friend's son. When Kyle's parents went away on a vacation, they left the one-year-old baby in our care. Once when checking out my groceries at a supermarket as I carried him, the clerk kept peering at me and then at Kyle who had white hair and very blue eyes. Curiosity overwhelmed her so she asked an indirect question, "What is his mother's nationality?" I said, "Swedish" and volunteered no more information. I'm sure I left her wondering why the child had not the slightest trace of Asian features.

When he was about fourteen, we took him to Camp Unistar, a family camp where Kyle and I had one week to visit. We took a canoe out to the middle of Lake Windigo and sat in the water while wearing life vests. It was just like sitting in a chair but being almost weightless. We had a chance to explore the purpose of life, why people are the way they are, what was important to him and what was important to me, and how to win at poker. For my eightieth birthday, he wrote me a letter about these experiences that caused me to weep with happiness.

Story Two: At Louise's memorial in 1997 in Minneapolis, a giant greeted me and then with a bear hug, lifted me into the air. While three feet in the air, I wondered who he was. It was Rik Hultberg whom I had not seen since he was ten years old. For a birthday greeting, he wrote about how we met thirty-five years ago. Once again this took place at Camp Unistar where he watched me getting my fishing gear ready to go fishing. He looked so interested that I asked, "Would you like to go fishing with me? Get your pole and let's go."

"I don't have a pole."

"Then use my spare rod. Get your lures."

"I don't have any."

"Then take any five that you want out of my tackle box."

"Aren't you going to pick them out for me?"

"No. If I did, I might pick something you don't like. Then it wouldn't be a gift, so you pick them."

Fishing was so good; we were able to feed the whole camp.

Story Three: For any organization to succeed, you need a few people who have the conviction to do whatever it takes to make the enterprise successful. Such a person is Vicky Wenkstern who worked for me as an executive secretary. For example, on a Friday night it became evident that what we had prepared for the CEO of the company was missing the mark; we had to redo everything. Members of my staff and I worked that weekend and then Vicky came in on Sunday afternoon and worked into the wee hours of the morning making our slides for the new presentation. She had them ready at 8:00 A.M. Monday morning when we needed them.

Vicky prepared entertaining documents for my birthday book citing the many wonderful times we had working as a team. I really appreciated her. She wrote stories of how I could never find my car in the parking lot and how I would wander out of my office in deep thought to get coffee without my shoes. New employees who didn't know me might have wondered, "Who is this character wandering around the halls without his shoes?"

When you have lived as long as I have and lived in as many places, you might acquire a ton of friends. I have five men friends, all formerly from Minneapolis, who go to an Elderhostel program somewhere in the U.S. There we play Oh Hell, mix martinis, flirt with the single ladies and exchange jokes and stories. When I return from these trips, I am refreshed and in the state of well being.

For the last twenty years, I have been going fishing in a remote part of Ontario, Canada that is accessible only by floatplanes. We gather in Minneapolis and then drive to Ear Falls, Ontario, Canada where we catch the floatplane to Lake Carroll. We do our own cooking and if anyone complains, he becomes the cook. Since it is such a large lake and so inaccessible, it has very little fishing pressure. We fish for walleyes, the best tasting fresh fish in the world. In our four-day trip, we might catch six or seven limits since it is a brainless kind of fishing that requires no skill. There I learned why people go fishing. For most, camaraderie ranks as the number one reason. The others are the preparation of the event, the anticipation of catching a big one, and the breathtaking scenery. Most of my fishing forays are disasters, so it is important for me to go to Lake Carroll to assure me that it is possible to catch fish.

As my readers know by now, poker is one of my great loves, so I play with a group of about ten men. We get together every two weeks at my home. We play whether I'm home or not. Over the last fifteen years, we've collected a strange set of poker games with names such as *Politician, Apollo 10, No Name, Killer* and *Shipwreck*. Seth Stevens, a newcomer groaned, "those aren't poker games." Gradually he got sucked in so he now initiates these games when it is his turn to deal. There's a lot of joking and story telling. In looking around the table, I don't see distressed faces even if they belong to losers at the moment. Attendance is high, for most of the men give these games high priority. Clint Sherman once asked me, "Why do you play poker?" I searched my soul and decided that it was camaraderie. In checking with the others, they agree with me and we are developing lifelong friendships.

Many years ago at the First Unitarian Church in Minneapolis, the board of directors had an open discussion with the members to find out why they came to church. The moderator pointed his bony finger at me and asked, "Carl, why do you come?" I answered, "I don't come here to absorb profound wisdom from the minister for that is an unreasonable load on the minister. I am not female enough so Women's Alliance is not open to me. I don't drink enough to need the aid of Alcoholics Anonymous and my wife hardly drinks so I have no need for ALANON. I come mainly because I like the people who come. I'm in tune with them, so a succinct answer would be, I come for the coffee breaks. Thereafter, guess what I became known as? Yes, I became known as the guy who came to church for the coffee breaks.

Tim Haley who worked at a hospice center for many years told me that people on the threshold of death never talk about wealth, success, achievements, or their physical beauty. They talk about their relationships with people. Though death is not imminent, the focus of my life seems to be my relationship with my wife, family and friends. Other things matter much less. Thus, I must conclude that life is rich for me because of the good people I know who come out to play with me.

Notes

¹ From page 70. A French villanelle typically has five tercets and a quatrain with the second lines having one rhyme and the remaining lines another and with the first and third lines of the first tercet repeated in alternation as the last line of the succeeding tercets and together as the closing couplet of the quatrain.

² From page 140. A Sestina is a lyrical form developed before 1200 by Provencal troubadours and now fixed in the form of six 6-line stanzas originally unrhymed, six end words repeated in different order in each stanza, and a 3-line envoi in which three of these six words occur in the middle and three at the end of the lines.

³ From page 161. A Sapphic poem consisting of a four line strophe of three primarily trochaic lines made up of five equal beats of which the middle is a dactyl and the others are of two syllables and followed by an adonic.

[4] From page 238. A Ghazal is an Arabic lyric poem that begins with a rhymed couplet whose rhyme is repeated in all even lines and that is especially common in Persian literature.

Carl Nomura was born in a box car in Deer Lodge, Montana in 1922. He was a child of poverty during the Great Depression. In the beginning, he was an indifferent student. One of his school teachers told him he should learn to work with his hands, "Take auto and wood shop," she advised. He took her words as a challenge. "She said I was a person of very limited ability so I should not take geometry and take the place of a more deserving person." Nomura said, "I made up my mind not to let her think that I was an idiot. I went from an *F* student to an *A* in Algebra."

He went on to master advanced algebra, trigonometry and solid geometry as well as Latin. He graduated from Van Nuys High School in Los Angeles in 1941, just in time to be incarcerated, along with all Japanese Americans in California. He and his family were sent to Manzanar—an isolated wind swept relocation camp—where they were held behind barbed wire fences, guarded by military personnel, and watched constantly by armed security forces in guard towers.

With this beginning Carl Nomura determined not to fail. After the war, he earned a bachelor of physics degree in 1948, a master of science in 1949 and a doctorate degree in physics from the University of Minnesota in 1953. He became a research physicist for Honeywell. But his greatest contribution came as an executive at Honeywell where he established one of the finest solid state electronics organizations in the world. He was hailed as a visionary leader in the field of semiconductors. He was lauded by his peers as "a scientist, a manager, and most importantly, a wonderful person."

We invite you to visit our e-zine, the *Yurica Report* at our web site at www.yuricareport.com for updates on our authors and for information on our latest books. The following Erasmus books are available at your local bookstore. They're unusual, poetic stuff. The kind of thing a rainy day brings out in a person: a desire to be left alone, yet wanting to reach out and be part of others who are making the same kind of journey.

The Lost Book of Wisdom by K.V. Yurica
Honey and Brine by Barbara H. Kaplan,